D1097514

The Art
of
Thinking

by Ernest Dimnet

A FAWCETT PREMIER BOOK

Fawcett Publications, Inc., Greenwich, Conn.

Member of American Book Publishers Council, Inc.

CONTENTS

CONTENTS

PREFACE

What writer would dare to appropriate Voltaire's verse in *Le Pauvre Diable,* and would dare to say of his reader:

Il me choisit pour l'aider à penser?

Yet, it is a fact that millions of men and women are anxious to take lessons in the Art of Thinking and that some other men and women have to take the risk of seeming presumptuous in offering those lessons.

Anybody who does it need not be a genius. Genius has never been supposed to be a particularly good teacher of any art. It is better that the teacher of the Art of Thinking should not be a person who knows no difficulty in thinking, or produces such brilliant thoughts that they will be disheartening to the tyro. A delicate physician does not give the example of health—any woodsman can do that—he only gives the example of a small capital of health intelligently increased: yet, we know he can be more useful from his comprehension of indifferent health and from his appreciation of hygiene, and we often prefer him. The author of this book is certainly not prepared to say that he has acted, or even is now acting, up to his own principles; still he is not bragging in saying that he has probably felt their value more than many people nearer to genius than he is. Is not this enough? And is not a keen desire to be of use a sufficient claim to give modest advice?

The reader will soon find that this book, whatever its shortcomings, has been written for him. Its effort at being lucid and brief, its aversion to philosophical jargon, its antipathy for a discouraging and generally useless bibliographical display, all come from a wish to help instead of dazzle. Most books are composed with the more or less avowed object of being works of art, that is to say of being an end in themselves and ultimately rousing admiration. Egotism, in writing of any art, especially of an Art of Thinking, would be criminal, and it can be honestly said it has had as little a share as possible in the preparation of this work.

It will be enough if the reader is conscious of sympathy to which he has a right, and of a continuous striving to help him in his effort to think his best and live his noblest.

The Art
of
Thinking

Part One

ON THINKING

Chapter One

ON THINKING

A FAMILIAR SCENE. Five o'clock late in October. The sunset over the reddening garden. You are standing near the doorsill, looking, and not looking, thinking. Somebody steals by and you hear the words whispered "a penny for your thoughts." What is your answer?

Later in the day you are deep, or seem to be deep, in a book. But your face does not look as it usually does when you are happy in your reading: your contracted brow reveals intense concentration, too intense for mere reading. In fact, you are miles away, and to the questions: "What are you thinking? What book is that?" you answer very much as you did when caught in that reverie, during the afternoon: "Oh! Thinking of nothing"; or, "Thinking of all sorts of things." Indeed, you were thinking of so many things that it was as if you had been thinking of nothing. Once more you were conscious of something experienced many times before: our mind is not like a brilliantly lit and perfectly ordered room; it is much more like an encumbered garret inhabited by moths born and grown up in half lights: our thoughts; the moment we open the door to see them better the drab little butterflies vanish.

13

The consciousness of this phenomenon is discouraging, of course. This accounts for the fact that, when offered a penny for our thoughts, we generally look, not only puzzled, but embarrassed, and anxious to be let alone not only by the questioner but by the question as well. We are like the puppy who is willing to bark once at his own image in the mirror and to snap eagerly behind it, but who, after the second trial, looks away in disgust. Yet, with some curiosity and some practice, it is not impossible to have, at least, a peep at one's mind. It should not be attempted when we are too abstracted, that is to say, when our consciousness is completely off its guard but there are favorable occasions. When we are reading the newspaper and the quickly changing subjects begin to tire, without quite exhausting us; when the motion of the train or of the car sets our thoughts to a certain rhythm which may soon become abstraction or drowsiness, but still is only a slackening of the mental processes; when the lecture we hear is neither good enough to rivet our attention, or bad enough to irritate us; then, and every time we are in a mental lull, is our chance to get a glimpse of our mind as it really works and as it reveals our innermost nature. By a sudden stiffening of our consciousness, a quick face-about inwards, we can, as it were, solidify a section of mental stream which, during three or four seconds, will lie ready for our inspection. If one succeeds in doing it once, one will certainly feel like doing it again, for no examination of conscience is so strikingly illuminating as that one, and the more frequent it will be, the easier, at least during certain periods, it will also become.

Why not do it now? A penny for your thoughts! What are you thinking of? . . .

You look up, surprised at what you regard as an exhibition of very poor taste in a writer.

"Thinking? Why, I am thinking of your book. You

may not be as interested in writing, as I am in reading it. I love this subject."

"Yes, I saw you were remarkably attentive; that's why I interrupted you. Had you been wandering, it would have been useless. So you love this subject?"

"I do indeed, and wish you would go on. Books should not talk."

"When you say you love this subject, you mean it interests you, it excites something in you; in short, it makes you think."

"Quite."

"Of course, these thoughts which occur to you as you read are your own, they are no mere reflections of what I am saying, and that is the chief reason for which you enjoy them as they rise from behind my sentences. Is it not so?"

"Very likely, Sir. I begin to like this conversation."

"Yes, it is about you; I knew you would like it. So, these thoughts which are your own and not mine are exterior to this book. Don't you think they could be called a sort of distraction?"

"It would be rather unfair, Sir. I assure you I am following you closely; yet, I must admit that I am not trying to memorize what you say: it would spoil all the pleasure I find in this. I am even willing to admit that my pleasure is my own and therefore might be called, as you say, a sort of distraction. In fact, I was thinking . . ."

"Ah! here we are! You were thinking . . .?"

"Well, I was thinking of a farm, up in Maine, where there used to be a garret like the one you spoke of. In summer, when we were there, the smell of winter apples was still in it, and I loved it. I would sit there for hours, as a boy, thinking. You see, after all, I was thinking of thinking. As a matter of fact, often when I see the picture which gives me the deepest impression of happy thinking

*—the portrait of Erasmus writing—I think of the old gar-
ret. I have no doubt that I thought of Erasmus, a few
minutes ago, for I was positively annoyed, for a moment,
at the recollection of a man who once stood before that
picture and asked me: who is this old fellow looking down
his long nose? I hate a fool. The memory of this one
actually made me fidget in my chair, and I had to make
an effort to think of something else."*

"You see that I was not far wrong; you have been
thinking of a number of things which were not in this
book."

*"Yes, but they came because of the book, and I should
not be surprised if I were to think of your book, remember whole passages of it, I mean, tomorrow while doing
important work at my office."*

"Thank you. Have you been thinking of that too?"

*"Why, it would be difficult not to. What I shall be
signing tomorrow involves a sum I might take five years
to make. However, I am almost sure that everything will
go well and I can buy poor Jim the partnership he wants."*

"In the meantime here's the penny I owe you. For
I begin to know your thoughts pretty well. Naturally they
are, every one of them, about you, and that is as it
should be. There are, of course, in your mind, thoughts
hidden so deep that no amount of digging up could reveal them, but there is no doubt that they would be even
nearer your *ego* than those you have discovered in the
course of our conversation. Sometimes, very unexpectedly,
we become aware of the tingling of our arteries in our
heads, even of the fact that we are alive; this consciousness is of no use whatever to us, unless it somehow concurs
in keeping us alive, but we are lavish when our Self is
at stake. Do not imagine that I am reproaching you."

*"You would be ungrateful, for let me repeat that I
have seldom read anything so attentively as this book."*

"Certainly. Yet, you must also admit that while you were interested in this book you were interested in something else. It is so with everybody. Have you ever heard that Sir Walter Scott, when he had found the nucleus of a new novel by which his imagination would naturally be engrossed, would, however, read volume after volume that had no reference to his subject, merely because reading intensified the working of his brain? These books did for his power of invention what the crowds in the city did for Dickens's. When you say that you were reading this book attentively, you mean that your intellect was expending some share of your consciousness—let us say one fifth or, at best, one third of it—on the book. But your intellect is only a sort of superior clerk doing outside jobs for you. You, yourself, did not cease for all that, doing the work of your Self, infinitely more important to you than any theory. What is important to you is the garret in which you used to muse away hours with the smell of apples floating around you, the picture of Erasmus which you love, your undying indignation at the man who did not appreciate that picture, your son's future and an exceptional chance of improving it. All the time you were imagining that the *Art of Thinking* was making you think, you were thinking of Jim, Erasmus, the fool, the garret and business, undoubtedly too, of dozens of other things we have not been able to trace back to your consciousness. Those thoughts, which you are tempted to call distractions, are what your Self is thinking, in *spite* of the book, and, to tell the truth, the book is your distraction. Even writing can be the same thing.—Shall I tell you what my Self thinks while the superior clerk holds my pen? It thinks that I should do my work with perfect happiness if, two hours ago, I had not seen a poor stray cat wandering in the drizzle with two frightened kittens at her side. I love cats as much as you hate fools."

Introspection, as it is called, looking inwards, while the mind is active, will always disclose similar things. Psychologists speak of the "mental stream," and this expression alone has meant an immense progress in the domain of interior observation as compared with the misleading division of the soul into separate faculties. In reality, the flux in our brain carries along images—remembered or modified—feelings, resolves, and intellectual, or partly intellectual conclusions, in vague or seething confusion. And this process never stops, not even in our sleep, any more than a river ever stops in its course. But the mental stream is more like a mountain brook, constantly hindered in its course, and whirling as often as it flows. When we look in we are conscious of the perpetual motion, but, if we do more than merely peep and at once look away, we promptly notice the circular displacement and reappearance of whole psychological trains.

These trains are invariably produced by some image in whose wake they follow. The gentleman with whom I just had such an enlightening conversation had his mind full of a multitude of images—inconsiderable reflections, as swift and also as broken and impossible to arrest as the wavelets in a stream—but he was conscious, or semiconscious of only a few. What were they? A room in a country house, the picture of Erasmus by Holbein, a fool, Jim. To change our simile—the more we use, the nearer we shall be to the endless changing reality—these representations were like the larger and brighter fragments in a kaleidoscope. To these the mind of the gentleman would every few minutes revert.

It is hardly necessary to say that these images acted upon him as all images act upon us. We are attracted by some and repelled by others. The old apple-room was altogether satisfactory; so would Erasmus have been, had it not been for that silly man, and, in time, even the silly man would have been tolerable because he produced not only irritation but a pleasant sense of superiority. As for Jim, it was delightful to see his not very good-looking face transformed by joy as he heard his father begin: "Well, old man, it's all right"; but it was the reverse to imagine him, a year from now, taking the same 8:17 train to do the same inferior work. Probably when the gentleman imagined he was smelling the shrivelled-up apples, happy Jim was behind the door, but when the fool's unforgettable six words were heard in that satisfied oily voice, Pelham station and the silent slaves streaming in with poor Jim were not far. I say probably, for who knows? Quite possibly, relief from an unpleasant picture was sought in a pleasanter one. The stream runs fast and so deep between its brambly sides that it is impossible to see anything clearly in it.

All we can say is: 1. That most of our mental operations are inseparable from images, or are produced by images. We do not differ in this from the dear animals near us. (If anybody does not realize that a dog's brain registers an encyclopedia of images, sounds and odors as large as a dictionary and far better remembered, the dog's behavior will be entirely unintelligible.) 2. That those images closely correspond to wishes or repulsions, to things we want or do not want, so that this wanting or not wanting seems to be the ultimate motive power in our psychology, probably in connection with elementary conditions in our being. 3. That inevitably, people will reveal in their thoughts and speeches, in their outlook on life and in their lives themselves, the quality of the images filling their minds. Investigation and estimation of these images, together with investigation and estimation of our likes and dislikes, will tell us what we are worth morally more accurately than even our actions, for they are the roots of action. But to this we shall revert later.

Surely, you say, what you have described so far is not thought. Our brain must be free sometimes from images, from likes or dislikes, from wants and repulsions. There must be a superior kind of mental operation, something immaterial resulting in abstractions. How are mathematical and philosophical systems evolved? What is logic?

Yes, there are languages abbreviating billions of experiences, and there are formulas filling whole libraries. The one of our savage ancestors, who, wrestling with onomatopoeia and almost in despair at seeing a shade of meaning which he could not express, for the first time invented the future tense by conglobing "to-morrow," or "sun-rise," or "morning hunger" with a crude verb-noun, was a genius; and intellectual work has produced libraries which, in their turn, keep the noblest minds occupied; and all this tends to abstraction. But the study of it belongs to the Science of Thought, while we are here concerned only with the Art of Thinking. Yet, it is useful, even for our purpose, to say a word about this less practical aspect of the subject.

We have an idea that thought—as diamonds are wrongly supposed to do—can exist in a pure state, and is elaborated without images. We feel sure that we are not infrequently conscious of conclusions, practical or speculative arrived at without the help of images.

Ah, What are they? But, first of all, are there any? How can we be sure that there are any? Every time we really succeed in watching our mental process we discover the presence of images. You say "thoughts," "pure thought," and you are persuaded that you say this without any accompanying image, but are you right or wrong? While you say "thought," is it, or is it not possible that you see a man's head, or his brow, or the inside of his head visualized, not as a horrible brain jelly, but perhaps as a more or less complicated wire frame destined to classify and keep in place the results arrived at, or as an infinitely delicate clockwork?

The names of mental operations which are now abstract were not so originally. To *see* and to *know* are the same word in Greek; to *ponder,* which sounds so intellectual, obviously means to *weigh;* to *think* is the ghostlike descendant of a much rougher word meaning to *seem; logic* and *speech* are the same word; so, in fine—as if to protest against too much intellectual pride—are *idea* and *image!*

Images can be subconscious and harder to detect than people who have not tried suppose. We can be conscious of one reel unrolling itself—with many crazy interruptions—in our inward cinema, and not be quite conscious of another fixed image, visible, but not easily visible, through the film. Nothing is more frequent than this superposition of two sets of images progressing with variable speeds. They account for the unexpected conclusions at which we arrive while apparently attentive to entirely different matters. A gentleman whose mind is occupied, while reading, with the tiny photographs his memory once took of a house up in Maine, may suddenly hear an inward voice say clearly to him: "It is very bad to read when you need not," and may shut up the book at once. Why? The process of solidification mentioned above would disclose under the Maine film the image of Dr. Wilmer, since the last visit hardly absent one instant from the subconscious. There would be three strata (perhaps more, of course) perceptible in the same consciousness:

Book on the Art of Thinking

House in Maine

Oculist

Sometimes we are aware of a succession of images driving, in fact, telescoping, one another toward a worded conclusion with extraordinary rapidity. The same gentleman whom I am sorry to have now made pathetic (but he will never go blind) may come to the unexpected conclusion: "I will buy that house in New Jersey!" Incredible! Not at all. The succession of telescoping images may be seen perfectly clearly:

a) House in Maine + slow trains + two changes + cold winters + Joneses near = not wanted.

b) House in Lakewood (recommended by agent) + good trains = near + no mosquitoes = sleep. Sleep + nearness + pine trees + sandy soil = attractive = smile = buy.

All these images may succeed one another with the rapidity of lightning, and, as we generally think of rapidity as a quality of thought, the concatenation will be called thought, but in reality it will only be a sequence of images, as usual.

Pretty often, we are conscious of isolated words vaguely obtruding while our mind is thus busy: they are like labels on the silks in a lady's workbox. More exceptionally, we see or hear a whole scroll of eight or ten words, as the gentleman did, and we are tempted to imagine we think in words, which would be superior to thinking in images. But we do not. The words and the scrolls are there from the habit which most of us have of sometimes audibly whispering: "plus seventy-five" while counting money, or "this must not happen again" when admonishing ourselves. The inner words are only an anticipation.

So, we are confronted with images, images, and more images. Abstractions, being the product of images, inevitably recall them. It is difficult to think of history without visualizing great men or some great period, and I doubt if we can mention science without remembering famous experiments. Few words, surely, are as spiritual as the word Truth, but when we hear it mentioned, we associate it either with some instance of devotion to truth, or with some particular search which makes us realize the beauty of truth, and, once more, definite contingencies reappear. Needless to point out how closely associated with figures even geometry is. As for logic, it means nothing if it is not pronouncing on congruousness or incongruity. Why should it not be the congruousness or incongruity of two images or clusters of images, accompanied by an abstract statement? In fact, we are constantly conscious that it is so.

It will be urged: but is there not in our mind something which is its very nature, and without which there would be no mind at all?

I see. You have heard of the principles of pure reason. Well, read the philosophers, and tell me if you are much excited, much enlightened, or much impelled to thought by being told that when you see a billiard ball send another rolling, your intellect registers that nothing happens without a cause or without sufficient reason. What Kant, or even a more practically inclined metaphysician, like Sir William Hamilton, tells us about the nature of the intellect may represent a powerful mental effort, but the results are not commensurate with it. We can catch a glimpse of the working of our mind, vague and not much more satisfactory than was the X-ray screen twenty years ago, but its nature must remain a mystery among many other mysteries. This idea, added to the fact that we are dealing with a practical art, and not with philosophy proper, should reconcile us to our ignorance.

Chapter Two

HOW TO ESTIMATE THOUGHT

THE QUALITY OF A MAN'S THINKING may seem difficult to detect on account of the various strata under which real thought generally is hiding, but, if introspection is applied, all the apparent difficulty vanishes. An experiment or two will make it clear that the criteria of estimation of a man's thought are, first, the images on which it exercises itself; second, the likes and dislikes corresponding to these images, and lastly, the mental energy which enables us to combine intellectual data with more or less success.

It is evident that a person whose mind is filled with the images of petty pleasure, comfort, good food, good clothes, dancing, traveling, amusing company, in short, material well-being, is farther away from what we call thought than the person whose imagination will be engrossed by beautiful scenes—Italian scenery, for instance—with noble fabrics, the quaintness or the appeal of antiquity, churches, and museums full of the realisation of beauty, and the recollections of great artistic lives everywhere. The superiority of an artist to a society man or woman who is nothing else is undisputed, and it comes from no other cause than the superiority of one class of images to another. Again, when the mind of a Ruskin or a William Morris is inhabited, not solely by images of sensuous beauty, but by visions of a better and happier mankind, we bow to nobler images than those which delight the mere artist. It is not difficult to go up the scale of moral values attached to magnetic images by visualizing in succession those characteristic of the patriot, the social reformer, the moral reformer, the saint or the great religious interpreter. These images become more and more sublimized, but they are as vivid to the mystic as to the artist. What visions pass through our mind when it is at leisure, what scenes do we spontaneously imagine? We should know, for the mere description of introspection is inevitably followed by an experiment. So we can be our own judges. The thought is rather formidable.

Of course, our likes and dislikes are of the same order with the images corresponding to them, and it would be tedious to dwell at any length on the subject. It is evident that any images of which we have no particular right to be proud would not be frequent in our minds if they were met with the verdict: not wanted, not liked.

On the other hand, attention should be drawn to the fact that most people are more conscious of their dislikes than of their sympathies. The latter are weak while hatreds are strong. It is one of the humiliating features of human nature that we resent a few little things which happen to irritate us more than we appreciate a great deal for which we ought to be grateful. A traveler's point of view can be modified quite unjustly because, during the last few days of his visit, he has been unlucky enough to meet bores, fools, or bullies. But sometimes he prefers meeting them because he enjoys grievances, and irritation agrees with him. A critic who feels like praising a book will gladly damn it if the last chapter antagonizes some pet idea of his. High-minded men and women endowed with warm natures are almost invariably optimistic, even when they realize the rottenness of the world, but how few they are! It is striking to reflect that Antoine, the Belgian faith-healer, made a European reputation by preaching love of our enemies—a doctrine so traditional (theoretically) for Christians. Thousands fortunately took it as a novelty and were enthusiastic in consequence.

Another symptom or cause of the pessimistic tendency is the presence in our consciousness or subconsciousness of the depressing mental habits which Freudians call *complexes*. We shall revert to them in the second part of this book but we must note them here at once because their effects cannot be overlooked in an estimation of the quality of our thinking.

Introspection can be supplemented and controlled by two sources of information which we can hardly hold in suspicion: our private letters, and above all our talk. Both are open to the full light of wide-awake consciousness and need not be investigated through the more psychological process. What are we hearing ourselves say? Are we satisfied with merely speaking the exterior or interior cinema? ("This car is going too fast." . . . "I wish we had a Studebaker." . . . "I feel quite ready for tea.") In the same way, are not our letters full of small talk and cheap details, different from the cook's only by virtue of a little more grammar and spelling? Does not our pleasure in criticizing rather than appreciating break out in many sentences beginning "I hate," "I detest," "I despise," "how I loathe" . . . and so forth? If so, we cannot help escaping the self-pronounced verdict: ORDINARY.

The third element to be taken into consideration if we want our inventory to be complete is mental resilience. Glibness, confidence, a retentive memory enabling its possessor to air easily acquired, sometimes shamelessly pirated, knowledge, can deceive observation at first, but not for long. As a rule, we can tell which of two men is the more energetic thinker as we can tell in a natatorium who is the swiftest swimmer. As for our estimate of our own mental elasticity, it is a matter of mere honesty requiring only the simplest investigation. If our mind is little better than the cinema mentioned above, we do not think any more than does a mirror. If we are bored by any topic above those which give food to our small dislikes or even smaller likes, we do not think. If, the moment a book or a newspaper raises a question demanding some supplementary information or reflection, we yawn, fidget, or hurriedly do something else, we abhor thinking. If, when trying to reflect, we at once feel a weariness, a drowsiness or a tendency to repeat mere words, we do not know what thought is. If we do know what it is, but, as Montaigne says, are too lazy to tackle a problem with more than "a charge or two," we are feeble thinkers. Then what are we really?

Copy-cats, humble slaves imitating their masters. When a traveller visits the United States for the first time he cannot help noticing a curious phenomenon. Americanization, the transforming of foreign dissimilarity into American conformity, is not done, as Americanizing centres imagine, by the substitution of a new set of ideas for another. The thing is done more simply. Long before the new arrival begins to know the language which he calls the American, and even before changing his name from Silvio into Sullivan, he is trying to be as American as his simple resources will let him. He shaves off his moustache and has his hair cut in the most military style. He goes to games and quickly learns to yell. Soon he begins to suppress the native vivacity on his face and replaces it by good-natured slowness. Nine times out of ten you will see him copy the hesitancy before speaking accompanied by a mute motion of the lips which is frequent in Americans of his class. He has no difficulty in adopting the salute with the hand which possibly America has borrowed from his Roman ancestors. He has been told, before leaving Naples, that a good American consists largely of good clothes, and his first money goes to that. He has no doubt that a country in which a boy of eighteen makes a hundred and fifty *lire* a day cannot but be God's own country. The notion gives him a horror for the smells of Italy. Shortly after this he has the revelation of the abyss there is between "the girls" and "le donne." By the time he can write home that he now speaks the "American" he is ready to make the world safe, at any cost, for democracy and the American woman, and he should be given his papers without another week's delay. The whole process has come from outside and its chief element may have been the mute motion of the lips which is a symptom of high receptivity.

What do most people do who are not poor emigrants but "people"? Do they not consist of clothes, fashions, mannerisms, formulas (listen to what you hear at the opera or at art exhibitions)? Are not only their attitudes, but even their attitude before life, copied from models approved for standardization? Are not their lives all alike?

Most of this questioning is superfluous. We know that nineteen people in twenty do not think but live like automata. I once reproached Mr. Arnold Bennett for entitling one of his books *How to Live on Twenty-four Hours a Day*. This title evidently suggests a book for hectic people in quest of a method to compress forty-eight hours into twenty-four. On the contrary, the book is destined for idle people and intended to make them live twenty-four hours a day. The real title ought to have been: "How to Live Twenty-four Hours," or "an hour" or "ten minutes" a day. For most people do not live even that long a day, and Mr. Bennett's book was worth writing.

Chapter Three

REAL THINKING

Enter thinker. We have all seen him standing amidst the surprised, incredulous and often silly group of non-thinkers. Sometimes he is a very simple man, the roadside mechanic slowly walking out of his garage. Round the car two or three men, hot with ineffective guessing are still talking excitedly when the taciturn man appears; for an hour they have talked, tried and failed. They stop and not another word is heard. The intelligent eyes of the artisan, helped by his seemingly infallible hands, go over the organs of the machine; meanwhile we know that his mind is going over dozens of hypotheses which to us are only riddles. Soon the trouble is found. Sometimes the man smiles. At what? At whom? I often wonder. At any rate we have felt the presence of a brain.

A score of medical students are standing round a bed: three or four of them have examined the patient and an interne is now doing it, for the case is exceptionally interesting and may go on record. Every now and then the young doctor says a few words which a score of pencils note down. But a flutter passes over the little crowd. The *patron,* Potain himself, is here. He has heard of this case and wants to see for himself. In a few moments his magnificent head bends toward the patient and a scene, unforgettable to those who once witnessed it, begins. Not a word. The splendid intelligence of the famous physician now abides in his ear. With closed eyes and a marvelous receptivity over his face, Potain listens. At intervals something like beatitude in his expression shows that this examination goes well: every infinitesimal sound, every absence of sound is interrogated: the students know that even a crease in the pleura becomes visible to this prodigious man as he listens. Half an hour passes without one of these young men getting tired of this scene, however mute, and entirely given up to thought. At last Potain reappears: the case is as clear as if all the organs were on the dissecting table—as, alas! they will be in a few days —and a few plain words describe it: through the solid thorax an irresistible intellect has done its divining work.

Do you know Cézanne's portrait by himself, a marvellous thing produced with such simple means that the artist might have found them on a desert island? If you have looked at it for only ten seconds, you will never forget the eyes, clear, hard, harsh, cold and sharp as steel. Artists often possess those eyes less made to love reality, as people say, than to go straight to its essentials. Degas had exactly that kind of eyes. Not very long ago, I saw those eyes in the head of a smartly dressed, dark-looking young painter, outside the "Ruche," in Vaugirard: he interested me and our glances were like crossed swords, high above the sphere of mere politeness. Those eyes see where others see not. What is the power of a Napoleon, even of a Mussolini? Not mere "power," but magnetism, and the magnetism is more intelligence than force. Such men *see,* they see the necessities of an epoch, and woe to the people who will not see them as they do! The contempt of the eagle for crawling creatures will fall upon them.

I remember once taking Angellier,[1] rather by surprise, to a drawing-room which the Quality was filling with the soft hubbub of elegant nothingness. He sat down and

[1] Auguste Angellier (1848-1912), professor of English Literature in Lille and Paris, critic and poet. His two volumes on Robert Burns and his sonnets *A l'Amie Perdue* are his chief titles to fame. His personal influence was extraordinary.

listened. Certainly he had a head which even conven-
tionality at its worst could not pass by, a superb head so
well poised on athletic shoulders that many people imagined the man was tall, though he was not. But, above all,
he had a power of attention, so visible in his deep sunken
eyes that it actually seemed to throw out a net on the exterior world. The disproportion between what Angellier
seemed to expect and what he was treated to, that afternoon, could not be left unnoticed, yet in a few minutes
the conversation became more substantial, every word of
it addressed to this unknown man with the expectant face.
Soon, too, the reward came. Angellier was seized by his
demon and gave us of his best: a succession of illuminating statements which his Shakespearean metaphors clothed
in magical brilliance. A rare spectacle. It recalled Angellier's own description of Robert Burns in the Edinburgh
drawing-rooms.

All great men, you say, all more or less famous men!
True, but is there a single human being who does not
know in his immediate vicinity a man or woman gifted
with a power of intellectual vision so superior to the average as to be striking? Is there a village where some
tavern star does not play the part acted by Branwell
Brontë in Haworth? Is there a single family, or little social circle, without its *tintinnajo,* the family oracle of
whom it is said, when difficult questions are at issue: Oh!
he will see the whole thing? Few conversations pass without our making the mental note: I had not thought of
that. It means that somebody, perhaps accidentally, has
been a thinker. Shortly after the Russian Revolution, in
1917, half a dozen people in a Paris salon were indulging
in the then familiar pastime of comparing the Czar with
Louis the Sixteenth, the Czarina with Marie-Antoinette,
Kerensky with the Girondists, etc., so that the future of
Russia could easily be inferred from the history of the

French Revolution. Somebody said: "Oh! you think the crisis is over, don't you? But what is that Council of Soldiers and Workmen which meets at the Finland Station? Wait; you will see what comes out of that." A brilliant intuition, which, in a few weeks, facts began to corroborate.

Such experiences are familiar to all of us and often leave a deep impression behind them. We love to see the thinker in action, for his personality, joined to the unexpectedness of his performances, acts upon us even more than the illumination he provides. Nobody denies that thought, like oratory, gains by being drunk at the spring. The Port-Royalists appreciated nothing in Pascal so much as what they called his "eloquence": to them the word did not mean, as it does to us, persuasive rhetoric, but a capacity for the ready expression of thoughts difficult to clothe in words. Probably their interest in the almost indecipherable memoranda left by the philosopher lay in the hope that these scraps of paper might revive the impression of his originality. Readers of Boswell do not doubt that Johnson was an extraordinary conversationalist, but how few students of English literature have a clear notion that a decade or two of the eighteenth century would never have been called the Age of Johnson had it been only for the *Dictionary, Rasselas* or the *Lives of the Poets?* Johnson's genius was in his talk and not in his books. As Léon Daudet says it, à propos of Marcel Proust, we love a conversation "full of flowers and stars," the stars being the rare thoughts and the flowers their fascinating expression.

Yet, from time to time, we see a thinker's ideas progress independently of him, either because the thinker was not eloquent, or because his ideas were difficult to grasp, or because the man himself remained nebulous to his contemporaries. This phenomenon cannot but give us an exalted idea of the greatness of thought. Measure Descartes, the refugee to Holland, or his disciple Spinoza, the artisan, or that typical provincial professor, Kant, or Karl Marx, by confronting their personalities with their influence. The contrast between those humble lives and the mental effervescence they have left behind them is startling. One flash through a human brain, and, in spite of a total lack of worldly influence, in spite of the recondite character of the doctrines, in spite of the absence of literary talent, the whole intellectual trend of mankind will be changed for several generations. Much more spectacular the process is when the man's personality is as powerful as his influence (Julius Cæsar, Napoleon), but it is not so extraordinary. Thought can indeed be called divine, for it is creative.

What is it that characterises the thinker? First of all, and obviously, vision: the word underlies every line of the descriptions above. The thinker is preeminently a man who sees where others do not. The novelty of what he says, its character as a sort of revelation, the charm that attaches to it, all come from the fact that he sees. He seems to be head and shoulders above the crowd, or to be walking on the ridge-way while others trudge at the bottom. Independence is the word which describes the moral aspect of this capacity for vision. Nothing is more striking than the absence of intellectual independence in most human beings: they conform in opinion, as they do in manners, and are perfectly content with repeating formulas. While they do so, the thinker calmly looks round, giving full play to his mental freedom. He may agree with the *consensus* known as public opinion, but it will not be because it is universal opinion. Even the sacrosanct thing called plain common sense is not enough to intimidate him into conformity. What could seem nearer to insanity, in the sixteenth century, than a denial of the fact—for it was a fact —that the sun revolves round the earth? Galileo did not mind: his intellectual bravery should be even more surprising to us than his physical courage. But, three hundred years later, it was no less difficult for Henri Poincaré to assert that there was as much scientific truth in the old notion as in Galileo's doctrine. Einstein's denial of the principle that two parallels can never meet is another stupendous proof of intellectual independence.

How many people, in August 1914, shook their heads at the world's certainty that the war could not last more than three or four months? Very few. Hundreds of people in Europe are trying to protect pedestrians from motorists; only one, that I know of, ever thought of the radical measure which alone would compel the motorist to slacken his speed: take away his Klaxon from him. Everybody laughs at the bombastic eloquence resounding in Parliament-houses, and obviously destined for some far-away constituency. There would be an easy method for greatly diminishing this evil, which would be to compel orators to speak seated, but who thinks of it? How many Americans realize that their country is not a democracy but an oligarchy, and owes a good deal of its stability to that fact? How many Frenchmen see—for it can be seen—the contrast between their modern architecture and the sublime or exquisite monuments scattered all over their soil? Indeed the world lives on words which it goes on repeating till some thinker, or repeated experience—*experientia magistra stultorum*—makes a breach in the solid and stolid wall of conformity.

People who think for themselves often appear haughty and self-satisfied, because they can hardly be dissatisfied with themselves, or irreverent, because they knock down idols and cannot but enjoy the sport. Men of the intellec-tual type of Mr. Bernard Shaw would evidently be sorry if all silly people suddenly became as wise as themselves. Hating folly and playing with it rather cruelly is a healthy exercise of the faculties: the Bible abounds with instances. Thinkers are also apt to appear dictatorial, to compel people to follow in their wake. The reason is because seeing the truth—whose other name is salvation—and realizing that other people will not see it, they treat them as grown-ups must treat children. Once more Mussolini can be used as an instance in point. But, in their innermost nature, thinkers are preëminently teachers, and it is to the credit of most of them that they devote their lives to preaching the truth they see. Some of them do so in admirable speeches or books, others in the picturesque language of the artist, but, whatever the vehicle, the devotion to truth remains visible. Some literary men appear original because of the bizarre character of their expression; but the least effort to boil down their most arresting page to its salt of pure thought will show that they have little to say: not being able to pose as teachers, they must be content with imitating the acrobat who makes a speech standing on his head while gesticulating with his legs. Such men will find imitators but no followers, whereas the thinker, whether he wishes it or not, is a leader.

Chapter Four

POSSIBILITY OF AN ART OF THINKING

W HAT IS OUR REACTION in the presence of a thinker? The same that we experience in the presence of beauty: we are surprised at first, but immediately after, we admire. Only, with some people admiration is accompanied by discouragement, with others it creates emulation. Purely literary people who think too much of brilliance are early dazzled by it into inertness. Average people react differently. The more confident almost invariably think: "What a shame that I should not talk like that! I might have. If only I had this man's chances, his education, his experience of travel, his connection with people accustomed to a higher kind of conversation, or only even to a better vocabulary, I should not be the dumb, dull creature I must appear to be." In their hearts, they think distinction is found, not gained, and they blame destiny. Others suspect under it all a recipe which they do not know but might learn. "Tell me how!" they seem to say, and entertain not a doubt that, if they were given the formula, results would immediately follow. Apart from the stupid listeners who regard a brilliant conversationalist much as a miserly old French farmer regards a generous American, that is to say, as a freak, people feel a kinship between themselves and the more gifted specimens of mankind. The only difference they see between the latter and themselves is accidental and likely to be effaced in an instant: in other words, they believe in an Art of Thinking.

Why do they? Simply because the most ordinary of us

know moments during which we glimpse the very states of mind which brilliant conversation mirrors. Anybody familiar with country people, even of the most uncultivated sort, realizes that they appreciate natural beauty, a landscape, the last smile of autumn on a wood, a sunset, the flash of a wild bird, quite as much as a professional artist or versifier. All they lack is words or oftener confidence; many of them are as loath to speak of their innermost loves as to change their accent.

Humdrum people cease to be humdrum when they hear a fine speech or read the kind of book likely to act on their dormant possibilities. Perhaps one human being in a thousand is absolutely impervious to the charm of music: the rest, no matter how crude, cannot hear Taps or *le Chant du Départ,* or a good organ, or a girl's song on a warm evening, without a beginning of intoxication which differs only in degree from the mental condition in which Shelley produced *The Skylark.* A tumult of seldom experienced and consequently more valued intellectual impressions, with the sensation of an unwonted warmth round the heart, are known to all men and women. We all treasure the recollection of such moments, and we never become quite so ossified by what is called life and its hardening influence as not to wish for their return.

Everybody too is conscious of spells during which his mind is at its best, works swiftly and infallibly. Insomnia, before ending in exhaustion, generally produces a lucidity which no amount of normal meditation will replace, and the vigils of literary men testify to the fact. Prolonged solitude accompanied by a little fasting acts in the same way. This too is known to all literary people. Dickens used to walk and walk through the streets of London in the small hours of the night when he could meet only sleepy policemen or stray cats. Most writers realize that their books are only written, not lived, when they cannot separate themselves from their families and seek the quiet of an old town or remote country inn where nobody speaks to them. Let anybody try the experiment of crossing the ocean on one of the quieter boats without making anybody's acquaintance. He will find, after three or four days, that his mind is not the same. The ten days', or even thirty days' silent retreats, in use in some religious orders, are the outcome of such experiences.

Were it even without the comparatively frequent recurrence of exalted moments breaking our routine, we could, all of us, be conscious of what is going on in the thinker's mind by recalling our childhood. All children under nine or ten years of age are poets and philosophers. They pretend to live with the rest of us, and the rest of us imagine that we influence them so that their lives are only a reflection of our own. But, as a matter of fact, they are as self-contained as cats and as continuously attentive to the magical charm of what they see inwardly. Their mental wealth is extraordinary; only the greatest artists or poets, whose resemblance to children is a banal certainty, can give us some idea of it. A golden-haired little fellow playing with his blocks in the garden may be conscious all the time of the sunset while pretending not to look at it. "Come along!" the nurse said to Félicité de la Mennais, eight years old, "you have looked long enough at those waves and everybody is going away." The answer: *"Ils regardent ce que je regarde, mais ils ne voient pas ce que je vois,"*[1] was no brag, but merely a plea to stay on. Who can tell what the four Brontë tots saw or did not see in the moors through which, day after day, they rambled holding hands? Cannot you remember looking

[1]"They watch what I am watching, but they do not see what I see."

for long spells at a mere patch of red on a sheet of paper
or in your little paint-box? Most intelligent children, as
was the case with Newman, have the philosopher's doubts
about the existence of the world. You see them looking
curiously at a stone; you think "children are so funny"
and all the time they are wondering if the stone may
not be eternal, and what it is to be eternal. Have I not
heard a little girl of nine interrupt a conversation of professors who were talking about nothing to ask the astound-
ing question: "Father, what is beauty? What makes it?"

This superiority of intellect persists until the child's imitativeness begins to work from the outside in. When Jack
begins to copy Daddy's way of shaking his head or shrugging his shoulders, his poor little soul also begins to be
satisfied with dismissing questions. Pretty soon this magnificent tide of interest which fills the child's soul will ebb
away to leave it dry and arid. There may be occasional
returns of it. All school-boys, writing an essay for their
teacher, are visited by thoughts which they realize would
be what is called literature, but they do not dare to write
them down, and ill-treated inspiration, in its turn, does
not dare to return. It is to those moments that such of
us whose vocation turns out to be literary look back with
despair, wondering what brought a crop of platitudes
where distinction used to spring naturally. Only in a Blake
or a Whitman is the passage from the child to the artist
imperceptible.

People forget their childhood, no doubt, and it is
a loss which, no matter how lightly they take it, is ir-
reparable. But, for a long time, they remember it, and,
more or less consciously, they try to relive it. It does not
occur to one in a thousand, of course, that he was more
intelligent when he was eight than now when he is fifty,
but it is no less true that the relationship we feel between
ourselves and even the man who dazzles us is founded

on recollections of great hours or on recollections of child-hood; "I have deteriorated" we rightly think; or "I am a victim, I have had no luck." Pretty often, too, we hear the inward admission immediately followed by a more hopeful feeling: "I am in a rut, I know, but if I would make the least effort, move only one line, say: 'hence-forth I will talk no more nonsense,' in an instant I could be outside of the herd of the unthinking to become one of the few leading it." A trifle, a mere nothing, the buzz of a fly or the bang of a door may be enough to disturb this mood and bring back commonplace thoughts in full force; but it is no less true that, during a few moments, we have been separated from a higher mental life only by a vision which we realized was within reach and by an effort which did not seem to be an exer-tion.

All this amounts to saying that we have a natural belief in the existence of an ART OF THINKING. Some men possess it, others not; but those who do not possess it must blame themselves.

Is this a real intuition? Must we really believe that the constant surging of thought and feeling in myriads of souls is as much of a waste as the useless effort of the waves? Was Gray right in thinking that:

> Full many a gem of purest ray serene,
> The dark unfathom'd caves of ocean bear;
> Full many a flower is born to blush unseen
> And waste its sweetness on the desert air.

Who can doubt it? Was not Robert Burns separated from illiteracy by the merest accident? Who does not see the element of luck in Shakespeare's life? Does not the life of Rimbaud demonstrate that a man can be two men? People who knew only M. Rimbaud, the East African dealer, in his counting-house, must have been astounded when told that this was Rimbaud, Rimbaud the genius, Rimbaud, who, before he was nineteen, had written immortal poems, but who despised literature ever after. What happened to Balzac? Here was a man who, between his twentieth and his twenty-ninth year, consistently wrote trash and, after that, produced nothing but masterpieces. Is it not evident to even a casual student of his development that the healthy working of his mind was hampered at first by the imitation of English novelists who had little in common with him, and only began to act freely when dealing with the data in his own experience? How can the historian of art or literature account for the marvellous growth of such epochs as the age of Pericles or the thirteenth century without exceptionally favorable circumstances preventing the waste of talent? Such periods testify to the existence, not of superhuman capacities in a few hundred individuals, but to that of a happy atmosphere helping the growth of the many. Medieval anonymity is another evidence of the diffusion of talent in those fortunate ages. Russians are supposed to have rare facilities for the acquisition of languages. Would it not be better to say that most nations look upon the acquisition of languages with a dread paralyzing the individual's possibilities? I have seen at least two French people, born in Russia, show the so-called Russian genius for languages, and an Englishman who never manages to learn more than a hundred words of Hindustani will not be surprised to see his children pick up three or four Hindoo dialects in the bazaars of Rangoon. Produce certain favorable conditions and you produce the Art of Thinking. The question is, how to produce those conditions, but it is not, by any means, a disheartening one.

Part Two

OBSTACLES TO THOUGHT

It is obvious that the chief obstacle to thought is stupidity, that is to say a congenital incapacity for thinking. However, no abnormal condition will be dealt with in the following pages. Most people who, in perfect good faith, tackle psychoanalysis, in the hope of bettering themselves, are repulsed by the fact that practically all Freudians seem interested only in medical cases. The man who has no reason to doubt that he is normal, but is conscious, like every one of us, of those obsessions now currently called inferiority complexes and wants to get rid of them, turns away in disgust from literature filled with hospital experience. This book is intended for average minds equally remote from genius which knows no obstacles, or from stupidity to which everything is an obstacle. It presupposes average lives finding the usual chances and encountering only the usual difficulties.

In the same way, no attention will be given to what is the main cause of human errors, viz: passion. It seems at first sight illogical to brush aside self-love, prejudice, and the innumerable likes or dislikes which prevent us from seeing even facts as they are, or inferring from them their natural conclusions. But the subject of this book is the production, not the guidance of thought, and its every chapter takes it for granted that we are honest in our wish to produce unadulterated thought.

Chapter Five

WE ALL KNOW THEM. We are all conscious of a double state of mind in which, behind a fascinating object, we see a threatening or discouraging phantasm doing its best to neutralize the healthy influence we would love not to lose. For instance, we see somebody we know engaged in a French conversation with a foreigner. How exquisite is distinguished, well-modulated French! What fluidity the loosening influence of the mute *e* and the nonchalance of the *n* sounds give to that language. Why, that girl seems to speak like a native. I had no idea she did. Not a trace of effort on her part, and that Frenchman does not seem conscious of talking with a foreigner. It is really wonderful. How absurd that I should have given up French! I still read it without much difficulty when I have to, but it is not often, and if I had to talk, I know I should be ridiculous. I really must do something. This very evening I will begin. Our French teacher used to say that if we would learn ten words a day, which is nothing, we should know almost four thousand words in a year, which sounds like a lot. Why should I not do it? Of course I will. And in a year and a half, I shall go to Tours or Grenoble to practise my four or five thousand words on harmonious natives. That's really worth doing, instead of going to silly plays.

Ten o'clock at night. Chardenal, the French Dictionary, Mérimée's *Colomba,* and an austere-looking vocabulary once bought in a hotel lobby are on the table. They do not look as attractive as that conversation sounded. Chardenal

46

does not look attractive at all. Yet, the grammar must be swallowed, verbs and all. Here are the four conjugations, not one less than last time the book was opened, and as merciless as ever. (*Enter phantasms as bad as phantoms.*) Of course, people with excellent memories can learn those verbs, but my memory is not good. Ten words a day is nothing, Mademoiselle used to say. Then, why is it that not a single girl learned them then, or has learned them since? Everybody imagined she would do it, but in fact nobody did. I have no perseverance. I have not even per-severance enough to reduce. I am not like So and So. No perseverance. So it is useless to try. Besides, is it so neces-sary that I should know French? Everything gets trans-lated, and, when Sorel or Guitry come over, you can al-ways guess a little and pretend a little. As everybody does it, and if I did know French nobody would believe that I did, it does not matter. After all there are other useful things besides French. That lecturer the other day pointed out quite correctly that we talk about Shakespeare all the time but read him about as much as the Bible. Let me read Shakespeare. One act every night should see me through in five or six months. I'll finish this trashy, amusing book I began last night, but immediately after I shall start on *Titus Andronicus*.

Memory not good. No perseverance. What's the good? So and So can do it, but I cannot. All these dishearten-ing little visions are what Miss Austen's characters used to call the "blues," not *idées noires,* but *idées bleu foncé,* not exactly obsessions, but parasitical obstructions. They all rush to the attack of a nascent volition and try to crush it out. If it shows a little fight in its desire to be-come a resolve, the hostile phantasms come back seven times more numerous and charge again till they firmly im-plant the inferiority complex: "I can't do it, it can't be done."

If we will indulge in a little introspection we shall find that our mind is peopled with more incipient obsessions than ideas, and that their presence is largely the cause of our impotency.

Inferiority complexes are not always the result of the presence of shadows like those I have just mentioned. It is sufficient that some purpose or desire, foreign to the thought or possibility of thought we are pursuing, should step in to arrest the process of effective thinking. Many people act in daily life a character not their own, and the working of their minds is hopelessly vitiated by the constant effort. Quite a few Englishmen, having trimmed their beards so as to look like Edward VII or George V, have never been themselves afterwards. Their thoughts, words and actions have been those of actors. I used to meet in Paris a man who looked miraculously like Alfred de Musset. But he was not Alfred de Musset, alas! and as he had persuaded himself he was no longer Dupont or Durand, he was nothing at all. Politicians frequently act historical characters and their natural insincerity becomes tenfold in consequence. People who begin to possess a language well enough to imagine that they may pass for natives, but have not really mastered it enough to use it as their instrument, can be frequently detected acting Italian exuberance, French vivacity, or British stolidity. Few students who have completely annexed a foreign language have escaped that rather ignominious phase; and they must admit that, as long as it lasted, their thoughts were not quite their own, but the reflection of some fancied Italian, French, or English type. One cannot exaggerate the influence of the English-American language in the Americanization of aliens.

Social intercourse with its requirements and its indulgence,—its hypocrisy, to call it by its name,— is highly productive of thought-hindering insincerity. How many people dare to say they have not read the book which three or four other people in a drawing room are discussing in non-committal language? How many are brave enough not to join in with an "oh! yes, charming book!" which does not deceive anybody, but which strengthens the soul-devastating habit of saying something when one has nothing to say. There is a quite as shameful *via media* between deceit and sincerity which consists in buying the book even if it is never to be opened. Casual inspection of some people's shelves is illuminating. The leaves of a certain category of favorites are uncut. I have no doubt that the success, not long ago, of one philosophical best seller was of the uncut description.

The same comedy is acted especially by callow young people who put on a profound air of having mastered it all. They affect the cant of sciences or arts about which they know nothing. What does one hear at picture exhibitions? It takes even less knowledge to display an after-the-concert appreciation summed up in "line, color and sonority."

The desire to appear, instead of really being, can vitiate even the legitimate operation of the intellect. Two men can be supposed, for example, to apply their minds with equal intensity to the question of the origins of the great war. If one of the two wants to display in his mastery of this question either his patriotism or his internationalism he will produce thought of a quality inferior to the other man's, whose sole object is to discover facts. The reason is that at every step onwards which he takes in his investigation, the former student sees himself using the information just gained, and the vision, like any parasitical phantasm, weakens, because it divides, his thinking power. Again, listen to a speech or read a poem with a view to remembering it: you will remember it better, no doubt, but your impression of the oratory or of the poetic charm will be diminished by such extraneous preoccupation.

Two notions juxtaposed in the mind invariably hinder its working. You do not see a picture as it really is when you have been told it is a copy whereas it really is original. The moment you hear that it is not a copy, the picture returns on you with an energy it did not possess a few minutes before. The only comparison that seems adequate is your surprise when you discover that what you thought was only a flaw in the window-pane really is a large kite in the sky: you actually see the tiny dot grow ten times as large as it seemed before. Exactly the same phenomenon can take place in our minds. We may have known a person, older than we are, for many years without realizing, one may say without seeing, his face: one day we suddenly see it and we are shocked to find it is an old face.

We live on notions and with notions. I have seen an intelligent and even, at times, scintillating man deteriorate long before his time, because he used at first to save every brilliant thought coming to him, for a better occasion, and gradually resent even producing such thoughts, as the torpedo-fish may resent discharging his electricity in the conviction that it must exhaust him. His registering every intellectual operation he was conscious of interfered with them all till, in time, he was a mere wreck. Methodicalness pushed to an extreme is well known to produce similar effects, because it becomes a haunting phantasm.

It would seem as if writers who are professionally trained to watch the operation of their minds, and in whose Mss. one is sure to find rich material for the composition of an Art of Thinking, ought to be freer than the rest of mankind from those blighting shadows. But it is not so. Most writers endowed with the real literary gift are nervous subjects, or at all events, exceptionally sensitive individuals on whose imaginations all impressions work freely and often cruelly. The Romanticists were proud of this sensitiveness and tire us by too frequent allusions to it, but it exists all the same, even in apparently robust intellects. In fact, it is one of the literary professional characteristics and is limited to the professional field. A number of literary people find relaxation in drawing and do so without any consciousness of their usual trammels. On the other hand, the careless and even reckless freedom of many artists, when they happen to write, frequently excites the envy of their purely literary brethren.

A writer is a man whose inner life is intended for public inspection. Unless he feel powerful enough to take this ordeal as a matter of course he is apt to think too continously of this inevitable exposition of himself, and the consciousness of it is a weakening phantasm. Nobody knows so well as the writer that he should not think of two things at a time, but nobody is more inclined than he to do so. Even that perfect collector of mere facts, that incarnation of unperturbed erudition, old Varro, has noted it. He actually says, in pithy Latin, that the man who informs himself in order to retail his information to others is a prey, while so doing, to an inferiority complex.

The writer is constantly beset with phantasms. Taine was haunted with a desire to hit upon an impossible world-mirroring formula, until the study of history cured him of this yearning by substituting such a simple summary of what history teaches us that, at first, the author was ashamed of it. A kindred phantasm is the fear of seeing only one aspect of the subject one is studying. Carlyle admits that he knew this obsession and had to make a desperate effort to overcome it. The writer is not afraid of mere critics—they belong to his own craft and he is ready to fight them with all professional weapons, including contempt—but he dreads the smile of imaginary readers, men or women, whom he has never met and who possibly do not exist, but whom he sees, in his mind's eye, as the realisation of all he would wish to be, mastering his subject as if they were giants. The obsession becomes worse when the formidable reader is known to be in the flesh. Most of Angellier's pupils have become writers: I have never known one who did not shiver at the idea of his master's good-natured criticisms, ruthless because they pointed out so infallibly the incompleteness of the disciple's outlook. Yet, Angellier himself was not always the olympian he seemed to be: the moment he thought of his own works he frequently showed anxiety or even depression, wondering at what height his inspiration really placed him, wistfully mindful not only of the greatest and strongest, but even of minors with a delicate handling of subtle nuances, dreading to be inferior to what he had felt himself to be in his first great effort, *l'Amie Perdue,* uncertain whether the subjects he was attracted by were in his best vein, and, during many years,—in fact, till he recovered some of his mother's religious belief,—staking his hope of immortality on the survival of some of his poems in the precarious memory of future generations.

Nobody can tell how many sterling literary vocations have been ruined by the notion that it is useless to repeat what must have been said many times in the past. Men like Amiel, or, before him, Joubert or Doudan, only escaped from this phantasm by writing things which they imagined nobody else would ever read. On the few occasions when they did write for the public, the cramping influence became visible at once.

The list of such influences hindering a gifted man's thinking could be endless. I cannot help adding that even a man as deliberately free from any clogging accretions as Jules Lemaître admits that the effort to visualise the past can become an obsession: its victim walks through the delightful quaintness of old Paris but does not see it: where the bookbinders of to-day sip their white wine of a warm afternoon, the obsession will show the revolutionary workmen of *Les Dieux ont Soif*, and the two visions neutralise each other. Many a Frenchman has never been able to recapture his first delicious impression of Paris, after reading the volumes of Marquis de Rochegude. Substitute Renan's or Signor Ferrero's mental habit of seeing the past as if it were the present, of speaking of the Roman *equites* in terms of Wall Street, and everything will be clarified in an instant; but the something which differentiated an *eques* from a banker, the spell attached to the distant past, will vanish.

The act of writing itself is productive of phantasms and is dangerous for the legitimate production of thought. Nobody ought to write who does not write with pleasure. But a number of professional writers are more conscious of an effort than of an enjoyment. Yet, self-expression is a joy to everybody and is often found to be a unique relief. The reason why it is not always so may be an imperfect command of the language used, or lack of real interest in the subject treated, or some one of the causes enumerated in the foregoing pages. But it is chiefly a phantasm acquired in school days, the habit of thinking of the blank sheets lying under the one we are writing upon, hating their breadth and length, and wondering how they can ever be all scribbled over.

Some people imagine they have to write a book as, at fifteen, they had to write an essay, whether they liked it or not. All the time they are at work on a chapter which ought to monopolise their attention, they are anxious over future chapters still unborn and even unconceived, and the anxiety throws its shadow over the page just being written. As long as an author does not take the habit of "only writing his book," as Joubert says, "when it is finished in his mind," or cannot honestly say, like Racine: "My tragedy is done, now I have only to write the verses," he will be a prey to the schoolboy's error. Nothing is as exciting as the hunt after thoughts or facts intended to elucidate a question we think vital to us, and the enjoyment of writing when the hunt has been successful is an unparalleled reward for intellectual honesty. Leave only the slavish necessity or the meretricious desire for producing a book and all the pleasure will be gone.

Some people who think freely and charmingly in speaking seem to put their minds in a strait-jacket the moment they begin to write. The wittiest man I have ever known, a French aristocrat, used to produce drab letters over which he would plod for hours. A former colleague of mine, with an entirely literary background, showed, however, an interest in philosophy and, without having read any of the philosophers, would discourse on the fundamental issues with surprising originality. "The Robinson Crusoe of philosophy," another colleague used to call him. This genius, every time he was compelled to write, relapsed into the state of mind in which he used to be, years before, when going through examinations at the Sorbonne. His own originality in thought or expression frightened him, and the results of his efforts, or I should say probably tortures, were cold, elaborate pages recalling dons' prefaces to dictionaries.

Most writers are slaves to certain models of expression. Millions of sentences might be curtailed of a final clause beginning with *and* which may be unnecessary as it is so often a mere repetition or summary added solely to round off the sentence. The habit of using three verbs or three adjectives where only one would suffice is almost as general. The average writer is not guided but coerced by a cheap rhythm as inseparable from him as the flute-

player was from the orator of antiquity. A man's thought
is hampered by these miserable toils.

More artistic writers cannot get rid of the notion that
the language they use is fatally inferior to the classical
style of past generations and, consequently, what they
produce is bound to appear as a monument of decadence.
They will not remember Goethe's well-grounded remark
that "the man who has been of his own time has really
been of all times." This thought would open the door
of the cage for them, but they go on knocking their heads
against the bars.

The writer the most cramped by adventitious preoccupations, impairing even a beginning of sincerity, is the art
critic. Compare Reynolds' *Discourses*, or Ruskin's *Modern
Painters*, or, in French, the absolutely honest manual of de
Piles with the articles on art appearing in most newspapers. You will feel at once that the so-called critics
only pretend to know what they are writing about, and
write about this negative quantity in an entirely artificial
style. It is always a surprise to me to see a forcible and
direct writer of fiction use, in dealing with pictures, a
cliché style which, in another man, would disgust him
by its effete far-fetchedness. The cause is that the novelist
transmuted into an art critic is not himself any more but
another man, and the double consciousness is like a man's
effort to see two objects at the same time.

Our mind then, is like our eye: it must be single. Children, plain people, saintly people, artists, all people possessed of a mastering purpose leaving no room for inferior
preoccupations, reformers, apostles, leaders or aristocrats
of all kinds, strike us by the directness of their intellectual
vision. On the contrary, timid, weak, easily abashed people, people made to follow rather than to guide, sensitive
people anxious about the impression they may produce,

doubtful of the working of their own faculties and everlastingly trying to get reassured, have a fatal capacity for
letting in extraneous thoughts or mental parasites, which
at first only obstruct but gradually obsess their own,
hampering their vision, and ultimately leaving upon them
that chronic sense of inadequacy which the term "inferiority complex" describes clearly, at all events to the
present generation. Had Freud and Adler done nothing
else but reveal the existence of such complexes and pop-
ularize the belief that proper treatment can dissolve them,
their influence ought to be regarded as beneficial.

HOW MENTAL PARASITES ARE PRODUCED

a) IMITATION AND GREGARIOUSNESS

I said in the first part of this book that all children enjoy
a few years of direct vision and immediate impressions
with which the most intense moments in their after-life
remain connected. This magical introduction to life can
be compared to the charm of dawn in the big city: during a brief spell everything seems as fresh as if it had just
sprung into existence, but the rumours and bustle of
the humdrum routine soon spoil even such a glorious
background, and banality sets in again.

Young children apprehend men and things without any
intermediary, and their first impression of them is so
strong that they need not go back to the original source of
impression. Hence the mistake many parents make in refusing to admit that childhood is observant. Towards the
tenth year things become different: children grow cogniz-
ant of their elders and copy them. In a few months, sometimes in a few weeks, you can notice the change: a little

man, a little woman, grown-up gestures, mannerisms in pronunciation or phrasing, a faked interest in certain things or a studied indifference to others appear; the expression of the face may not be affected, but it ceases to be spontaneous. Boys are more inclined to put on a rough, I-don't-care look,—sometimes worse, if they happen to be in coarse surroundings; girls, on the contrary, recall the thirteen-year-old brides whose mature conversation and artificial letters the seventeenth century used to take for granted. In many cases the observer fails to notice any conscious effort on the part of these aspiring grown-ups, but he cannot help being aware of a marked decrease in spontaneity and charm. The ideas expressed, the attitude before life, sometimes even before grief, are uninteresting or unpleasant. Soul resilience is inferior to what it used to be. You will see boys of twelve or thirteen take stolidly their first experience of the ocean, of the Canadian forests or of Rome or Egypt. Altogether these young beings who, up to a quite recent day, had been like just-born clouds in the summer sky, feeling every breeze and catching every reflection, now are all passivity. As the years glide on, if no noble passion helps them to climb up to the hill brow again, they will look more and more like the multitude, lazily borrowing their thoughts, attitudes or language from the millions.

What is to be done? It is the whole problem, for what can save a child from conformity would also empower any one of us to produce thoughts of his own. Children have to be educated, but they have also to be left to educate themselves. In America it is in vain that parents are naturally inclined, and schools are more and more advised to allow children all the mental freedom they can use; conformity is too strongly established and it takes genius to escape from it. In France, and practically in all the old countries, imitation and a certain amount of insincerity are recommended. "Look at your father—do like father—think of others and not of yourself—let them talk; they will love you if you do—do not always say all you think; you will give offence and people will not like you." There is no doubt that the model proposed for imitation is not Alceste but Philinte. And certainly Philinte is no fool; there is, well hidden in him, a strain of irony which belongs only to a correct appreciation of mankind, but who can deny that Alceste sees realities of a higher kind?

It is needless to say that, given what the world is, most children are more unfortunate than lucky in their surroundings. When they are poor, and feel badly dressed, badly brought up, and generally inferior, no matter how distinguished their intellects may be, they will be apt to be browbeaten into conformity. When they have stupid parents their questions, if they reveal any originality, will be misunderstood and laughed at. It is not unheard-of either that religion, the mainspring of man's rising above himself, is used by children's elders as a method for crushing them into conformity. Should they glimpse the fact that Christ and the saints did not conform, they will pretty soon be made to realize that Christ and the saints are in a world apart, and good little children ought to be satisfied with doing what they are told to do. So the combination of the natural instincts of man for imitation with the antipathy of the multitude against distinction, almost inevitably grinds thought out to leave only the human gramophone.

Gregariousness is an instinct nearly akin to imitativeness and tending to develop it. Nowhere is it so apparent as in the United States. It may be that the early pioneers brought with them the aptitude for coöperation natural to the Anglo-Saxon race, but could not, for a long time, use it because of the comparative solitude in which they had to live; the consequence was that they were predisposed to give it full play as soon as they had a chance. At all events, their descendants are the most social people on the planet. French people in towns as well as in villages, meet on Sundays, *à la sortie de la grand'messe,*—a distinctly social expression—but after devoting ten minutes to questions complementary of the all-round scrutiny during the sermon, they retire to their *quant à soi.* Americans never have enough of one another. The Club is insufficient and has to be supplemented by midday luncheons, meetings or gatherings of all kinds, changes of officers or initiations, a reception to this or a memorial ceremony to that, stag or hen parties, to say nothing of concerts or the theatre which are only pretences; and, when nothing better offers, your social American will make the most of a hotel lobby or of the "smoker" which I should be ungrateful to mock, for I owe partly to it my knowledge of the American man's few faults and numerous qualities. The word "joiner," which in England only designates a carpenter, means in America something purely American, as the sound of it,—as affectionate as sarcastic,—intimates.

It is well known that democracies produce uniformity. So do social miniature democracies. Too much individuality there would amount to not playing the game. When people form an association to protect common interests or foster common tastes, they must be expected to develop and encourage similarities. Attitudes are created, standpoints are emphasized, slogans are circulated which place a uniform imprint on people otherwise different. Dissenting where there is so much that can be promoted only by union, would be worse than heretical and is practically impossible. Mental resistance is hardly less so. The waves which sweep over communities in times of great excitement or great calamities blind and bewilder all except the most powerful. But the unseen continuous influence of the collective consciousness produces the same results. I have been amused several times in the United States to find transplanted countrymen of mine showing the same prejudice against negroes which prevails around them, but of which they had no idea before emigrating. Here is no attitudinizing; gregariousness in all its degrees makes individual thinking, viz., the only real thinking, an insuperable difficulty.

Examples in point could be adduced by the hundred. There is no more striking evidence of the power of gregariousness than our attention to the divisions of time. The almanac and the clock reign supreme, and if they should disappear, civilization as we know it would collapse. But, while we are enabled by them to catch the train and to cash coupons, we are also their victims. Not only do the active little seconds, in Maupassant's phrase, nibble away our lives, but, every year, another birthday falls on us like a rock, while the idea of age, as opposed to youth, is a gigantic phantasm. Oscar Wilde says that the tragedy of old people is that they feel young; that is to say, they really feel as young people would if some wizardry made them imagine that they were old. There is no evil spell here, but only clocks, calendars, and A.D.'s on every human document we touch. If these could be removed, things would change at once. Think of the delightful smile of the old Maryland negress whom you foolishly ask about her age. She has no age. But it costs a white man an effort amounting to genius to think away the fallacy of anniversaries.

Fallacies are every day produced by ignorance or imperfect knowledge, and are instantly circulated by the press. Their presence is a positive static. It makes thinking an impossibility until facts demonstrate that the apparently satisfactory notion was the result of inadequate information. People say that wars are inevitable till a League of

Nations is founded; then they say that peace can no longer be disturbed—until the failure of a Disarmament Conference causes them to adopt another formula. A terse sentence is enthusiastically repeated by people eager for some classification of the facts they witness. In a few days this sentence may be transformed by the press into a slogan with a whole train of practical consequences behind it,—who can tell how many divorces have been brought about by the "pursuit of happiness" being mentioned as an elemental right in every American child's text-book of the national history?

b) EDUCATION

Is it not paradoxical, to the extent of being in bad taste, to speak of education as an obstacle and not as a help to thought? Is it not a fact that we can tell an educated man from another, not merely by his manners and language, nor even by his information, but chiefly by his capacity for resisting another man's thought and defending his own views? Is it not true that we are never surprised, when we meet a brilliant young man, to hear that he received his education at one of the great English public schools, in a Paris *lycée*, or at a famous German or Polish gymnasium? Practically all philosophers, from Plato to Herbert Spencer, include an Art of Thinking as well as a treatise on education in their philosophies, thereby implying that the two things hang together. Horace Mann and Channing have produced in the United States a vast progeny of men convinced that they can only raise the democracy of their country up to real consciousness by education. The more a man thinks the better adapted he becomes to thinking, and education is nothing if it is not the methodical creation of the habit of thinking.

Precisely. Theoretically, education is a mental training

aiming at greater intellectual elasticity, but the question
is whether education does not often strain, instead of train,
a mind. Are people generally satisfied with the education they have themselves received or see dispensed to
their children? Are they not complaining about it all
the time? It is remarkable that Rabelais, Montaigne,
Locke, Fénelon, Rousseau, as well as most of the numerous
educators who appeared during the nineteenth century,
are *against* teachers. It may be because most of these
theorists never had any experience of that wild unbroken
thing, a class, and imagine that what they now are they
already were at twelve or fourteen. But it is chiefly because their superiority of intellect traces the shortcomings
they are conscious of to bad methods of which they were
the victims in childhood. Teachers who—quite rightly—
pooh-pooh reformers possessed of the foolish notion that
a class is something else than an undisciplined young
colt, agree, nevertheless, that current methods of teaching are not good. Their controversies, the tests and statistics they use to prove their points fill libraries. This being
the fact, it is difficult to resist the conclusion that education is not the Art of Thinking it ought to be.

However, our point is that it can be worse than this.
At an age when impressions are as deep as they are in-
sidious, uneducating education can produce mental parasites which, in time, are apt to result in inferiority complexes, or—a worse evil—can distort our whole outlook
on life. In every country education has its faults which
it would take libraries to discuss. We must limit ourselves.
But it will not take long to show that education in the
United States is too resolutely practical and leaves in the
pupil's mind the phantasm that culture is the privilege or
the amusement of a few; whereas education in France is
precisely the reverse and places culture at such a height
above action that the mere pleasures of the intellect seem

immeasurably more important than the practical duties of life. In both cases the capacity for right thinking is impaired and a lifetime may be necessary to correct the initial mistake.

Education in America is still largely an education for pioneers or the sons of pioneers. This affirmation may surprise people living in the giant American cities, yet, even there, traces can still be found of pioneers' ways or pioneers' ideas. The haphazard method of indicating the names of the streets or the numbers of the houses, sometimes on a bit of plank rescued from some wreckage, is an obvious survival. So are the solitary letter-boxes on the ends of sticks in the most civilized parts of ultra-civilized Long Island. And I have no doubt that the notion so prevalent in the United States, and so fruitful of consequences, that women are scarce, is a relic of the days when women were really scarce and the emigrant who secured a wife crowed like a Roman youth bringing home a Sabine girl.

The American schools are mostly in the country, because primitive American life was a country life and the Pilgrims had seen the schools at home located in small towns or in open suburban quarters like Westminster. And they are schools preëminently intended to develop physical strength and its spiritual counterpart, will-power. Where the ancestors used to fell trees in the vicinity of dangerous Indians, and with an eye on the ever-ready fowling-piece, the boys of Groton, St. Mark's or St. Paul now develop superb bodies, a capacity for fending for themselves, a passion for camp-life and an independent spirit to which the instinct for coöperation adds rather than detracts. Sports are still, and often avowedly so, the essential part of the school life. I have not forgotten that, on my first introduction to one of the above establishments, I was taken almost at once to the cupboard

in which glorious baseballs rest on silver rings, and respect-
fully made my ignorant salaam to these fetishes. School
news in America is sport news. Notre Dame is a Catholic
college, certainly, but it is that much less than it is a
stronghold of football.

To be sure, athleticism is partly an art. Women frequently enhance it by elegance and, when they do so,
should they be as ignorant as Saxon princesses of the seventh century, they achieve an artistic result. But athleticism is not culture, and the complaints continually heard
in America about education arise from the impossibility
of reconciling too much athleticism with culture. People
often ask me: "Why do your young men seem to know
so much more than ours, and use it so much more effect-
ively in their conversation?" I am always surprised to see
them stare when I reply: "Because school life in France
means getting up at five o'clock and studying till eight at
night with only two hours recreation in between; because
travailler in French means to study, where as 'to work'
in English applies to 'work' on the football field or on the
river. Our boys have mature brows but narrow chests;
yours have broad shoulders but childish expressions."—
"Is there no golden mean?"—"Yes, you will find it, and
plenty of it, at Smith, Vassar, or Bryn Mawr, or in that
perfect Thélème, the Princeton graduate school." "Ah!
you do me good. Your boys are narrow-chested, eh?"—
"Yes, till they have served a year or two in a regiment;
we love to see them there, not merely because they are
keeping up the national militarism and bloodthirstiness,
but because the army gives them a chance of broadening
their shoulders."

The predominance of sports in schools, in the national
life, in the press, not only crowds out what is or should
be more important, but it creates an atmosphere in which
these important things are made to appear superfluous, or

are even described in extremely disrespectful slang. What does seem important is a bustling, hustling life, with the excitement of getting in or out of a scrimmage, beating somebody or something, getting there. All of which is, within its limits, an excellent way of looking at life, but is not culture. Angellier once asked a student which tragedies he preferred, Racine's or Victor Hugo's. "Hugo's," was the reply, "there is more life in them."—"More tussle," Angellier mused, half to himself. Thoughtfulness, which is the highest form of life, is reconcilable with tussle only in a deep biological sense which is too subtle for this practical book to enter into. The plain fact is that the boy who shows the greatest activity or initiative on the game field is not by any means always the one who asks the most intelligent questions. Frequently he asks no questions at all, and his attitude is the "Tell us" which Madame de Maintenon used to hold up to contempt to the Saint-Cyr girls and which some American college professors have told me is likely to be retranslated in American college English into the blunt: "It's *your* job to tell us." A school is a place through which you have to pass before entering life, but where the teaching proper does not prepare you for life. What is called culture is in danger of being regarded, in such an environment, as a specialty and not as an indispensable requisite. Scholarship might be calculus. This accounts for the fact that the American public at large, which cannot bear the idea of foreign superiority in anything else, does not care a fig if it is beaten in the field of thought or of the arts. Who worries if one's neighbor is better than one's self at weighing the planets? To what extent this indifference is carried can be measured from the fact that an American newspaper *never* tells its readers whether the speech it reports was a good speech or not. Oratory is a specialty; only facts interest the millions. Yet, Americans love eloquence.

I have often amused myself by imagining Cicero suddenly appearing in America and being interviewed at the Hotel Biltmore by two newspaper men, one French or British, full of school reminiscences and beyond himself with excitement at the thought of seeing the ORATOR; the other, an American, rehearsing questions concerning prohibition or spiritualism, and really wondering if the Acheron is now crossed by motor-boat, or whether the Elysian Fields are properly gridironed.

To sum up: the notion of culture is too often dimmed in the American mind by the phantasm, uselessness; and thought, with such an impediment, is difficult indeed.

Has it always been so? Is this a part of the American idiosyncrasy which cannot be modified? Anybody who has disturbed the files of early American newspapers or reviews does not hesitate to give this question a negative answer. America is constantly spoken of as a young nation or a nation of young people. I used to be on my guard against this formula which I thought might be only an extensible lid covering all boxes. Gradually I have come to the conclusion that it is largely true. But it is true only of modern America. Early America was not young; it was quite mature. Not one of the men who signed the Declaration of Independence would have struck a member of the contemporary English Parliament as unduly young. The contrary would probably have been the fact. But not one of those men could appear on the campus of one of the modern successors of their Pennsylvania, Virginia or Maryland schools without shrugging his shoulders at the seriousness with which mere play is now taken. America has grown young during the latter part of her career, but this youthful America is something different from the historic United States. The American élite knows and deplores this. The extraordinary effort towards the diffusion of education seen everywhere in America is the vital reaction of a society feeling itself threatened in its essentials. But the resistance of the unwieldly mass, so far, is too great. The requirements of this mass still fashion the educational methods instead of the mass being fashioned by them, and no amount of testing, trying, or theorizing has, as yet, been able to change this preposterous situation. The mass wants easy methods, and so the methods are easy. It wants immediate practical results, and practicality is considered first.

Easy methods seem to be a dogma with Americanizers. Easy is the word one hears all the time in connection with the art of teaching. I wrote, a few years ago, a school-book which was published in New York under the title *French Grammar Made Clear*. The book has been misquoted, scores of times, as *French Grammar Made Easy*.

French grammar cannot be made easy. Nor can Latin grammar. It can be made, and ought to be made, clear and interesting. But no attempt at brightening it with Alma-Tadema pictures can conjure away the declensions, conjugations and modes. The best psychology is to persuade the pupil that hundreds and thousands of not very intelligent people before him have conquered those dry beginnings by mere perseverance. In fact, little peasants trained for the priesthood by plain country *curés* who never dream of calling themselves scholars constantly master Latin morphology in three or four months. More than once I have seen the neighboring clergyman drop in during the lesson and play with the *petit latiniste* as the Tuileries *enchanteur* plays with the sparrows. Seldom does the red-faced little fellow miss a crumb of the cases or tenses slyly flung at him. No inferiority complex with regard to mere words has been planted in him. He does not think of his declensions as something difficult or something easy, but as something which everybody has to learn and does learn.

On the other hand, read the directions issued by the New York Board of Education concerning the teaching of elementary Latin. The person who drew them up was evidently full of the notion that everybody must think Latin morphology as uninviting as the cuneiforms, and all that can be done is to take it in easy, i. e., minute instalments. Several months are supposed to be necessary to master the first three declensions; then a long rest is given to the student as if to prepare him for a final and much worse spurt; then the last two declensions are tackled or, I should say, played with.

What psychological background is likely to be created by this nerveless method? Evidently a notion that the Latin declensions are a nightmare, but *dies* and *cornu* are more formidable than the other three. My own teacher, who had no idea of any directions but who possessed a tradition, said to us in perfect good faith: *"Dies* and *cornu* being simplicity itself, you shall learn these two declensions, instead of one, for next time." The result was that even dunces were not afraid of the Latin declensions. Ask most American boys and girls who have gone through a classical course, and you will find that Latin morphology is as vague in their minds as badly taught Greek is in Europe. People in America remember being put through a book or two of Cæsar, a book or two of Virgil, an oration or two of Cicero, but their idea of Latin as a language is that it is a University specialty, as Sanskrit appears to most people, i. e., something you are not expected to know. My surprise was great when I saw an American poet who shows no small pretensions to scholarship entitling one of his poems *Pueribus!* Such are the results produced by making Latin easy.

The real result is that four, five or six years of so-called study only leave the impression that "nobody knows Latin; nobody can know it." A deeper and more dangerous one is that giving time to such a hopeless task is an absurdity. The suspicion that to compel young American citizens to go through an entirely useless routine is absurd and even immoral is not far. Try to play the Tuileries *enchanteur's* game with one of these school boys. You will read a great deal in the bored or incredulous expression; either an inferiority complex is there, working its usual damage, or it has already been kicked out, along with ancient wisdom, by a young barbarian who refuses to be made a fool of.

Utilitarianism in education is as disastrous to culture as so-called easy methods are to scholarship. The preference for scientific branches which can be turned to immediate account is of course a manifestation of the utilitarian spirit. So is the purely practical teaching of modern languages prevalent in most schools. So is the absence of all philosophical teaching in the High Schools.

But more striking is the way in which apparently disinterested literary efforts are turned to mere utility. I was quite impressed the first few times I was shown a school paper, and realized that a staff of boys under a boy editor was responsible for what is comparatively excellent stuff. It was only by degrees that—in spite of the poems which Anglo-Saxon boys or girls produce with more facility than French students—I realized that here was, not a literary, but a newspaper training. The school newspaper is a good newspaper but that is damning praise, for a good newspaper is not literary and a school newspaper ought to be preëminently that. The editor ought to have in mind Addison, Cobbett or Bernard Shaw when he writes an essay; as a matter of fact he does not even think of Mr. Mencken's imitators: the little home paper is his standard of excellence. If Addison were imitated the results would be poor but literary; as it is, the results are not literature, even if they seem fair.

The same can be said of the short stories, one-act plays
or scenarios produced in the Fiction or Drama schools of
many an American college. The teaching is first-rate, the
methods are far more thorough than those used in the
classical courses, the wish to succeed and the effort towards success cannot be questioned. What are the results?
Undoubtedly superior in craftsmanship to, say *Wuthering
Heights*. The terseness, the rapidity, the turn of the wrist,
the balance, impress and almost intimidate you. In time
you discover that these qualities are the accompaniment,
or even the creation, of an ardent desire to produce a
"marketable" article. Then you understand why the more
you read of those excellently manufactured stories the
less claim they seem to have to be called literature. Literature is not so clever. It wrestles with life and often gets
beaten, but the struggle compels our homage. Anybody
who has received a literary education feels this; but if
education goes over to the enemy and begins to teach
commercial methods, the minds, even of the *élite,* will be
invaded by the parasite of utility at all costs, and the
power of thinking in terms of beauty will lose in consequence.

The American boy leaves school with a more or less
definite idea that what is called culture is a luxury, that
is to say a superfluity. He has not been taught to view Latin
as an artistic mosaic, or English composition as an effort
to rise above himself. His imagination has been discouraged rather than cultivated. He is far inferior, in cultural
respect, to the Americans of eighty years ago.

In absolute opposition, French schools turn out young
people convinced that nothing, except the attainments of
intellect, has much right to respect. Educated French men
and women, with whom deep spiritual realities do not
act as a counterweight, find it difficult to take a practical

view of life because of a phantasm created during their formative years: the self-sufficiency of the brain.

Nine out of ten French schools are located in towns. The most famous ones are in Paris. Many of them still use ancient monastic buildings as different as can be from the château-like schools of America, and these medieval monuments are, in many cases, the successors of Gallo-Roman schools. A tradition of culture handed down through many centuries clings to these grey walls, but the very sight of the cramped courtyards shut in between tall houses betrays a disregard, nay a complete ignorance, of bodily requirements.

Many Frenchmen still alive knew no other exercise in their school days than the dismal circuitous walk allowed to prisoners in penitentiaries, and twice a week the melancholy walk through the suburbs and back. The early recollections of such writers as Taine, Daudet or Bourget are full of self-pity. But they admit that, while their bodies were inactive, their minds were busy: these poor boys' vitality was kept up by the excitement of discovery in thought or expression and the clash of ideas, which make French conversation something like an adventure.

Today the *lycéen* goes regularly to the "gym," and on Sundays or Thursdays he actually has a chance of playing football or tennis. But his daily routine still shows two hours given to play as against eleven given to study, and the French champion on the game field, if he happens to be dull elsewhere, will be an object of amused wonderment rather than of admiration.

School in France does not mean boys, it means teachers and books. For centuries the books were the Latin and Greek classics taught in order to be spoken, or at all events written, as naturally as the student's mother tongue. Little else was drawn attention to, but the characters of ancient history became familiar, and the main lines of the science of politics were inferred, even when they were not taught.

Today literature has routed all its rivals, even science, no matter how idolized, and it is so in schools as it is in life. Greek, Latin and French classics stand on the school-boy's desk beside scientific books and manuals of history. But the one book to which he will naturally revert, the one which his hand instinctively seeks at vacant moments, is his Lanson or his Desgranges, the manual of literary history. He may have a turn for mathematics and know he must face years of severe effort before he can get ad-mission to the Ecole Polytechnique, but literary history will be no less attractive to him.

What does he get out of this panorama of intellectual development elsewhere almost exclusively reserved for grown-up specialists? A mixture of good and bad. He certainly acquires a philosophical bent by noticing the concatenation of ideas, systems or sentimental reactions which make up the history of literature: his mind be-comes used to the logic of facts, and, year after year, grows more enamoured of the lucidity resulting from the vision of causes and effects. But, long before he has had time to do more than take a cursory view of the great monuments of literature, he has been given general ideas about them. He has acquired the terrible French craving for summing up complex realities in one formula, and too often he has grown accustomed to the semi-philosophical jargon of the literary historian. If he is mentally strong, his vocabulary will be helpful; if he is not, the learned words and apparently illuminating fore-shortenings will only give him a cheap superiority over people who have not had his training. They will give him something even worse: insincerity. For, in his heart, he knows that he says a great deal for which he would be unable to give chapter and verse.

Even more frequent is the French boy's delight in reading about a writer's personal development. The Romanticists, especially, from Rousseau to Loti, ravish his soul. The possibility of living a life rich in emotion and made sublime by inspiration seems to him the one desirable goal. Read Fromentin's novel, *Dominique,* if you wish to realize the havoc wrought by such a huge obstacle placed at the outset on the path to right and sensible thinking.

Is this exaggeration never corrected by French teachers? you ask. A French teacher, in Paris especially, is unlikely to dispel this fallacy, for he himself is a prey to it. Count the masters in English and especially in American schools, who publish books. How can they, since when they are not with the boys, teaching, they are with them playing? A French teacher is a man who has written, is writing, or wants to write a book, quite possibly a novel or a play, and to whom literary renown is the one glory worth working for. His example, as well as the point of view he cannot help expressing, contributes to plant ever deeper in his boys' imaginations the phantasm that literary men and women are the real heroes. The word genius is repeated in French schools till the pupils cannot escape from the double conviction that it is the one thing worth having and that they will never possess it.

Living incarnations of genius the French boy eagerly seeks. Sooner or later he will Boswellize one of his own discovering. In the meantime he delivers himself up to the influence of his teacher, sometimes of the top boy, a French institution of which no Steerforth can give an idea. I do not think that the scornful French vocabulary cruelly distinguishing between the *tête* of a class and its *queue* exists in any other language. It predisposes the wretched *queue* to humble subservience to what is wrongly supposed to be superior and diminishes its self-respect. In other countries sporting achievements, daring, or some promise of business sense or executive ability will give those so-called inferior boys a feeling of strength which saves them; but in French schools intellectual superiority is unchallenged, and the corresponding inferiority complex is at liberty to fill the soul it has once invaded.

Practical consequences in the life of the nation itself are only too visible. The passion of the French for ideas makes them imagine that when an idea has been expressed, its own virtue will be sufficient to get it realized. Properly analysed this fallacy can be reduced to the notion that some practical person will do what we are too superior to undertake. Hence the everlasting vision and brilliant *exposé* of reforms accompanied by a caustic denunciation of abuses so striking in French conversation. I once took a foreign visitor to the house of a friend of mine where social improvement was the business of the *salon*. This extremely earnest young man was impressed to the highest degree. "A lifetime," he said, "would not be enough to carry out all the plans this two hours' talk has disclosed to me as possible." The Sunday after I gave him the same treat. Not one of the possibilities which had seemed so urgent a week before was as much as alluded to. A brand new set was produced and passionately discussed. The young man was astonished and I was a little anxious about his next reaction, for earnestness does not flourish in the vicinity of brilliance.

Foreigners who make in France a stay of sufficient duration to be personally affected by the numerous shortcomings in the official life of the nation are invariably puzzled. How can such intelligent people put up with such absurdities? they ask. In time they give themselves some sort of an answer. I have not forgotten the verdict which, when I first visited the United States, in 1908, a famous American politician passed in my presence. "The French are bright," he said, "but they are not intelligent." It was a comfort to reflect that the word "bright" in American-

English is marvellously extensible, but I felt the sting of truth. Abuses are tolerated by the French provided they can laugh, or make cynical remarks about them. The press campaigns, the enlightenment drives which are persevering ly carried on in the United States are impossible in France.

The toleration by the French of their politicians is of the same order and arises from the same feeling of superiority of ideas to mere contingencies. Politicians are despised as roguish valets are by indolent masters. The Scandinavian idea of compelling them to be trustees for the community, or of expecting tangible results from their presence on the boards of the national administration, never occurs to the average Frenchman. Life, he thinks, is not very hard, after all, even if governments do not try to make it perfect. Good-humoured contempt is reform enough.

Preference for ideas, especially general ideas allowing simplified visions, is a French trait, even when terrible consequences may be the result. An Englishman, practically all the time, an American, in most cases, will know when positive danger to their country, and consequently to themselves, is imminent, and promptly cease discussing ideas to see to practical measures. To dance on a volcano is a decidedly French phrase describing a French attitude. Ideas count more in France than facts, and as long as education is at one with the national bias to prefer the art of living to the struggle for life, this one-sided view will go on.

Let us now remember our little boy of nine or ten, so receptive that great poets envy him, and so full of searching curiosity that philosophy cannot keep up with his questions. What becomes of him when he leaves school? In America a husky young chap, all muscles, heart and wishes; in France a slender young man, all brain, totally unprepared for life, apt to mistake ideas for realities and words for ideas. Both have received their education, both have had their chance. The American will always remain ill-equipped, full of intellectual gaps, uncertain between confidence and timidity and showing it; the Frenchman, if he is not saved by his religion, by patriotism or by some other uplift, will be largely artificial. Both men will think the thoughts of their environment, not their own, and education, which is nothing if it is not an applied Art of Thinking for one's self, will be to blame for this result.

Chapter Six

THOUGHT WEAKENED BY LIFE

a) THE THINKER'S LIFE

People are wont to praise life as the great educator. In fact, nobody can deny that life is a succession of lessons enforced by immediate reward, or, oftener, by immediate chastisement, which cannot pass unnoticed. Our successes and our failures create in us an instinct for safety which we decorate with the names of experience or wisdom. It is also a fact that action, when it is of certain quality and calls forth our best energies, acts upon us as our noblest experiences may, and we look back to the few years or months during which the effort lasted with a nostalgic yearning. To some men the word "Front" means the place with the sublimely vague name where their soul was at its fullest. . . . On this high level, action not only can help thought, but it produces it with a continuity which raises it to the height of creativeness.

However, these are rare experiences, and it cannot be denied that daily life, the apparently tremendous effort of one thousand million mortals repeated day after day, adds little or no thought to the common capital while, on the contrary, it wears out the individual's thinking capacity. Plato says: "Experience takes away more than it adds; young people are nearer ideas than old men." Young saints are not scarce, an old one is a delightful exception. We cannot dissociate solitude, freedom and leisure from our concept of a life dedicated to thought: Spinoza in his one room where the carefully chosen monotony of

77

his manual work acted on him as the monastic routine acts on a Benedictine scholar; Descartes leaving Paris for a quiet suburb of far-away Hague; Bossuet retreating like a hermit to the cabin at the end of his garden; Pasteur or Edison in their inviolate laboratories; learned monks in their convents; sages in the shady seclusion of a Massachusetts village; artists everlastingly trying to form colonies uniquely dedicated to disinterested work: all show us pictures of the kind of existence we imagine as naturally favourable to thought. The social life they conjure up is reduced to a minimum. It is little more than a soft accompaniment to the working of the mind, as the hum of the spinning-wheel is to Marguerite's reverie. We must feel some life going on near us, and even an occasional dip into exaggerated activity is a tonic, but social intercourse should never be more exacting than that which we have with the watchman protecting us during our nights.

b) NON-THINKING LIVES

Over against the calmness, security and concentration of the life of a Spinoza, set the existence of most of the people we know. They speak of themselves, rich or poor, as driven slaves, drudges, who "cannot call their souls their own."

Millions are oppressed by manual work, either because there is too much of it, or because the life has been taken out of it by standardization, or because its alternate praising up or depreciation by so-called labor leaders replaces their natural attachment to their occupation by uncertainty and sometimes hatred. Many hundreds of thousands who would feel inclined to think highly of their work and realize its dignity cannot indulge the tendency because of the insecurity in which they live. When you see the traces of untimely weariness on a man's face, in nine cases out of ten, you may be sure that overwork is not to be blamed; what is to be blamed is the anxiety of not having any work to do; that has sunk the eye and pinched the mouth. Literary or artistic people with a vocation and no means are the classical instance and well deserve to be. After they become famous their historians are apt to repeat the thoughtless and heartless saw that it is good for writers and artists to be a little hungry. The fact is that wealth is injurious to art, but artists cannot live without a certain amount of success. Failure and anxiety have never been known to elicit the best from a man's faculties. Too often they have done the reverse. The man seeks refuge in misanthropy or in dissipation. If he tries the usual path to success, endeavours to make himself agreeable or popular, curries favour with rich or influential people, he loses his dignity, and the quality of his thinking deteriorates simultaneously.

Driven, slaves, and drudges are also the rich. Preachers and moralists are apt to say that rich people are less happy, have more cares than the poor. I heard a bearded Capuchin once say that golden crosses were heavier than wooden ones. These metaphors sound well under the vaults of a cathedral, but they are not true. Golden crosses large enough for one to be crucified upon do not exist; if they did they could be sold for big sums and the price of them given to charities. Rich people have fewer cares than poor ones—that is the sober truth—but they are driven by their fellow men and women, drudges to organized nothingness, and slaves to amusements. Their endless complaint is that they never have any time and are glad occasionally to be sick, in order to steal a little rest. Yet, they dread solitude and their one antonym for amusement is boredom. Travelling teaches them something of the outside appearance of the world, and social life gives the best gifted of them a store of facts—though it is surprising to notice how little they know about human nature. But time for thought they have not, a taste for serious conversation or serious books they seldom have or soon lose. They live on their most elementary instincts, seeking happiness in pleasure, affairs, or power.

Whatever they do, they try to sell oftener than they buy, not realizing that in the life of sentiment egotism gives us the shadow for the substance. Soon their scale of values is falsified, immediate fruition taking precedence over unknown deeper joys. A worldling is pre-eminently a person whose judgment is not right, because his mind is full of inferior images and tyrannical phantasms. And gregariousness is the most powerful tyrant in such lives. People, still more people! Often distinguished men or women appear in the drawing-room or at the dinner-table. But of what use are they beyond the petty satisfaction of saying: "Oh! I know him"? Who listens to them? Who helps the hostess in her effort to give the lion a chance? Who wishes to make the most of a rare intellect? On two occasions I saw Cardinal Mercier pitifully wasted. Americans cannot realize how many chances for mental improvement they lose by their inveterate habit of keeping up six conversations when there are twelve people in the room.

To sum up, the child notices grown-ups and begins to think their thoughts; he goes to school, and too often education imposes other people's thoughts upon him instead of helping him to go back to his own; once out of school, he makes money, or arrives, or amuses himself; there is no question of thinking any more, unless we call thinking using one's mind to attain practical ends. Altogether, life does just the reverse of what it is supposed to do; it travels away from thought, and the process begins when we are ten years old.

c) **THE GREAT WASTE**

Reading is supposed to help thinking; a man who reads simply borrows another man's thoughts, and this means a craving for thinking. A scarcity of books is understood to amount to intellectual fasting. Reading, Bacon says, makes a full man; and Dangeau, dining with Louis XIV, once answered a question of the King with the sentence: "Reading does to my mind what your Majesty's partridges do to my cheeks."

But there is reading and reading. The word, like "intelligent," like "wit," has been in service a long time and its fringe has gradually become different from what it used to be. Reading, in its earliest stage, cannot have been remote from a magical or a hieratic process and was part of a rite. Our way of reading by just running our eye quickly along a page of type would have surprised and shocked the Ancients. Few people, in antiquity, knew how to read, and few possessed the bricks, stones or rolls necessary for reading. So, like Herodotus at the Olympic games, they were expected to impart to their less fortunate brethren something of the treasure in their hands. Reading out loud seems to have been the rule. It must long have been the custom even in private reading, and the rustic who moves his lips as he reads is keeping up a tradition. Candace's eunuch, who was reading Isaiah on the Gaza road, would not have been overheard by Philip had he not read his book aloud. A biographer of Saint Ambrose also tells us that this learned archbishop was sorely tried in old age by having to renounce reading, "because his throat was affected." So people would only take up a book for a purpose and with a gravity now reserved for reading the Bible or documents of a semi-sacred character. The whole soul was in requisition and its whole power, undiminished by distraction or by phantasms, was applied to the high task. Who can doubt that reading, under such conditions, must be effective? Legouvé, a mere man of the world, once beat Cousin, a philosopher and a scholar, in the discussion of a doubtful passage of La Fontaine. Cousin asked the reason, and the other man said: "I always read La Fontaine out loud whereas you read the *Fables* as most people do; my voice tells me when there is a danger of misinterpreting a line."

So the quality of reading was excellent.

The quality of what was read was as good. Books were few and costly and there was no idea of accumulating them indiscriminately. Even the invention of printing did not at first modify the composition of libraries: religious books, poets and philosophers were the foundation; light reading was provided by Homer or by the historians. The libraries of Kings and those of the rich monasteries seldom counted more than a few thousand volumes. Individual collections were naturally smaller. Spinoza possessed less than sixty volumes, of which we have a list. A hundred years later Kant collected three hundred, but half of this number were narratives of travel, for Kant had a frivolous side.

People, from necessity, as well as from a traditional choice, limited themselves to what we call today the classics but in those days were simply called good books. They were mostly written in difficult languages which it was not enough to play with, as our students do today, but which must be mastered. Latin had to be spoken, and even Greek was still used by Petavius when he defended his thesis at the age of twenty-four. The *Thesaurus Linguae Graecae* of Stephanus is full of echoes of Greek conversations held in the printer's backshop. The scholarship of those days tackled everything with a decision which was the very negation of an inferiority complex. If you studied one volume, you knew the sacred writings of the Christian religion; if you went through the few tomes of Aquinas, you knew theology; if you annexed the *Pandects* you knew law. The effort was made by thousands who thought no more of it than a modern apprentice to an electrician thinks of his hourly approach to the mastery of his trade. Every minute counted.

It is not surprising, therefore, that many men were supposed and supposed themselves to be in possession of practically all the knowledge of their day—a belief destructive of all phantasms. It is not surprising either that men whom we should call young and immature were regarded with unalloyed respect. We now speak of men of forty-eight as young. This is a purely modern notion bred of the fact that wisdom has now to be forced upon us. The men of the French Revolution were never derided on account of their youth, as the men of the Commune, eighty years later, were. Guy-Patin, telling in 1660, the amusing story of the feud between the physicians and the surgeons, relates that the former were defended by M. Lenglet, professor of rhetoric in the Collège du Plessis, and rector of the University. He subjoins that this remarkable orator was a native of Beauvais and twenty-six years of age, but he attaches no more importance to one particular than to the other. A man of twenty-six was a man and not a boy, as we foolishly imagine and openly say, to the detriment of the race by the diffusion of a dangerous phantasm. If he began early enough, worked hard enough, and worked under the best conditions, a man of the pre-scientific periods felt himself thoroughly equipped before he was twenty-five.

Today printing has gone mad and the world is in danger of being submerged by the ocean of books. Eleven thousand volumes are annually published in France alone to about seventy under Louis XIV. And who can think, without feeling dizzy and sick, of the billions of words deluging every Sunday morning the American towns? "Make your own choice!" the guilty editors would say. "Know what you want! We have it ready for you." A wise counsel, indeed, for the whole Art of Thinking is in it, but only the man who knows how to think can follow it. The others, millions of them, will be awed or bewildered by the formidable inroad of printed things upon them. In such a confusion, phantasms and inferiority complexes germinate like microbes in an active solution. The worst of them is probably the notion that one cannot have an opinion about every book, yet one must seem to have one. This gives a free field, and secures a multitude of slaves to slogans. People pretend they have read what they have not read and repeat anyhow somebody else's judgment. Nothing, of course, can be so destructive of thought and of the capacity for thinking. No such lever can wrench a man from out of his own soul.

When people do read, what do they read? Certainly not Aquinas or the *Pandects*. Many pretend to read the Bible, but of how few it is true! Three or four in a thousand read poets: they are regarded with the same surprise—not unmixed with mistrust—with which the poets themselves are considered. What is produced by the gross, what is constantly forced on our attention, trumpeted by publicity and magnified by criticism is fiction. Novels fill the bookshops and suffocate our bookshelves. What people read in the country where there is a little time to read are novels; what people pretend to read or skim through in town where there never is any time are novels. And the novels are not those great works of fiction which, since the sixteenth century, have added to our knowledge of mankind, or even their modern successors of such fame that we cannot ignore them; they are, and the readers know they are, pure and simple trash, the very titles of which will be forgotten in a week. "What are you reading?" I once asked an English friend, a woman of high character and no mean achievements—"Novel."—"By whom?"—"Don't know." (*Semi-guilty, semi-apologetic little laugh.*)

Novels are read to kill time—the most sacrilegious phrase in modern languages. And the word "read," since the people of the past three or four generations have been weakened to death by fiction, not only has lost its former majesty but has changed its very meaning. It is now mentioned, along with smoking and playing cards, as a semi-physical relaxation; the notion of a definite purpose in giving one's self up to it is excluded. The real purpose hidden under the gregarious act of reading is NOT TO THINK.

This is quite plainly visible when the time-killer is using periodicals. I do not mean the reviews or even the magazines. Anybody who, in default of books, has lighted in the country on a forgotten nest of the *Revue des Deux Mondes,* or *The Atlantic Monthly,* or even of *The Saturday Evening Post* must have realized how much substantial food is canned in those apparently ephemeral objects. Moreover, I shall have a chance in the third part of this volume to draw attention to the capacity of the daily newspaper to transform itself into a first-rate instrument of thought. But it requires a special need, a special gift, or a special education to raise it up to that level. In most cases the newspaper is not read at all or is barely glanced at. Often it is still neatly folded up late in the afternoon until the maids feel they must give it a chance. Or the way in which it lies over an armchair is revelatory of the kind of attention it has been vouchsafed.

The true measure of its possibilities as a thought-weakener is taken when we watch an average newspaper reader in the train. I remember once observing a man on the other side of the aisle between Philadelphia and New

York. We both had the *Philadelphia Ledger* across our knees. I made a few red marks on my copy and then began to notice the gentleman. He read the account of the swimming feat accomplished by some lady in the Hudson River. This was a story of some length which had to be continued on page 6, column 3. But the gentleman was unequal to the effort of turning three big sheets over; he was reading, not exerting himself.

So, leaving the grease-coated nymph, he went on to the cross-examination of the Pig Woman in the New Jersey case, and, dazed by the fusillade of irrelevant questions which the Pig Woman herself described in an immortal sentence as "talk, talk, chatter, chatter," he began alternately to fidget and yawn, but he never skipped a line. The whole mortal newspaper was read through in that way, on the brim of disgust or sleepiness, with occasional flickers of energy accompanied by a stiffening of the bust and a falcon glance at nothing through the window. In time the swimming lady reappeared in a corner, and the Pig Woman filled serried columns again, and there was a presidential message to Congress, and editorials, and news of the corn market, and shipping and sporting intelligence. All this was read on the same level, and with the same unfathomable disinterestedness till we neared the tunnel. Then the gentleman, all fagged and faint, showed a marvelous reflex; he flung down the crumpled sheets, jumped to his feet and felt for his cigarettes. He had been reading.

Imagine the effects, in the long run, of a so-called intellectual process which consists in presenting to the mind a score of different objects in none of which any real interest is taken. If we remember that our most serious attempt at mastering what we read is constantly hindered by adventitious images which we call distractions, leaving possibly two thirds of our consciousness available for what

we read, we shall have little doubt that reading, as prac-
tised by most people, is nothing but a method of not thinking. Let this go on for several years and the brain will
become what is properly termed jellified. Now, this goes
on through a whole lifetime with the majority of men
and women. They leave school or college at eighteen or
twenty-two. At that stage academic necessities have compelled them to read mostly serious books and to read
them seriously. As far as education goes they were going
in the right direction. The first thing the world and its
so-called civilization do for them is to persuade them that
masterpieces are tedious, text-books or encyclopædias boresome, whereas light literature goes along with freedom.
Henceforth reading will be one of the destructive forces,
arrayed against them. The newspaper, above all, will bewilder them by its desultoriness or weaken them into faint-
hearted common scepticism by its contradictions. They will
be the toy of irresponsible head-liners.

Here let me conjure up, only for an instant, the wistful
face of the man immersed in business, thinking of intellectual culture as of a Paradise Lost, and able at most
to devote half an hour a day to religious or philosophical
reading, or occasionally to a poet worth the name. How
noble and pathetic this visage looks! How we bow to the
often marvellous results produced by the thirty minutes
set aside for thought! But how rarely we encounter the
almost heroic person who will save himself from annihila-
tion whereas millions happily plunge into it. The idea of
such a thing as printing contributing to such a result is
well-nigh unbearable.

Another waste—so well known and unfortunately so
inevitable that it is useless to say more than a word about
it—is conversation. "Conference makes a ready man,"
Bacon said. Ready for what? The Ancients, like most
Orientals today, seem to have spoken only when they had

something to say, and their scale of valuing what was worth saying and what was not, appears to have been the same as that of their best writers. Hence the pithiness of their speeches. When a writer, not even of the highest order,—say Mr. Galsworthy—hits upon the device of contracting his dialogues to the two or three brief sentences with which impassioned people will wind up a conversation, he produces an unexpectedly powerful effect.

Now, think of the twaddle in the "smoker," of the empty boyish tongue-wagging in club-houses, of the *risqué* gossip gilt over with a dash of wit in French salons, or of the corresponding Anglo-Saxon delight in stale anecdotes! What a mockery to repeat that speech is the instrument of thought when it has become the mere satisfaction of a physical craving! If Bacon should rewrite, in the light of modern facts, the famous sentences from which I was quoting above, he would say that reading despoils a man of his personality and conference shows that he has lost it.

The general conclusion of this Part II can only be melancholy. Man is born without phantasms or inferiority complexes and with a capacity for observing and garnering thought-fostering images. Life, including such—apparently—helpful influences as education and literature, destroys this tendency, as an April frost kills blossoms, and imitation, ignoble conformism, takes the place of originality. Mankind is like Herculaneum—covered over with a hard crust under which the remains of real life lie forgotten. Poets and philosophers never lose their way to some of the subterranean chambers in which childhood once lived happy without knowing it. But the millions know nothing except the thick lava of habit and repetition. A small section of people tells them what they are to think and they think it.

Part Three

HELPS TO THOUGHT

Chapter Seven

LIVING ONE'S LIFE

a) EXTERIOR SOLITUDE

Many people fear it and call it depressing, a selfish or immortal, few really prefer it, but almost everybody thinks of it with pleasure. The name has a beautiful sound which even the hackneyed Latin jingle: *o beata solitudo, o sola beatitudo!* has not succeeded in spoiling, and the idea is enchanting. We envy Madame de Sévigné leaving the Court and her friends for the retirement of her Breton manor, Bossuet or Meredith alone in their hidden cottages at the end of the garden, Rousseau in his forest, Silvio Pellico in his prison, Alain Gerbault on his ocean-bound boat. Dickens among his friends charms us in Forster's volumes; why are we even more attentive when we hear of his endless rambles through the streets at night? The picture shows us nothing except a man in quest of we know not what in the dark, yet we are fascinated by it more than by anything immediately available.

The fact is that even the most worldly worldlings get tired of the nothingness of their lives, and know the surfeit of sameness. Although they play the game with a bravery worthy of a better employment they feel beaten sometimes, and relieve themselves with the profound complaint that "they cannot call their souls their own." They hanker for solitude, even if it is only a few days in Paris in Summer or in Newport in the Spring. They cannot always afford it; then the semi-isolation of the concert, of a simple service in an unfrequented church, or a few hours in the auto relieves the intolerable pressure.

There is in every man a feeling of enmity to things—whether they happen or only exist. We hate the crowded, confused lumber-room where no motion is free, we want to push rubbish out of our sight, to reduce objects to a minimum, as the Carthusian does in his white cell with just a plain black cross on the wall. The notion of vacuum is repellent to us, but let enough appear round us and above us to create the idea of a shelter and we breathe freely and happily. We "find ourselves," as the phrase goes, our poor neglected self, dearest of friends, yet dragged along everywhere like an ill-treated dog, hardly ever spoken to or taken notice of, going where it listeth not, till at last the unnaturalness of it all appears, and, for a few hours, we live instead of just being alive.

The Art of Thinking is the art of being one's self and this art can only be learned if one is by one's self. Society only produces social thoughts, *vulgo* slogans, that is to say, words, but words endowed with the power of a command. Solitude produces an exhilaration of consciousness, the consciousness of our innermost, whatever that may be. It never fails of this result. Take strong coffee one morning, to keep yourself awake, lie not in bed but on a couch for two or three hours, and try to simplify and again simplify your problems, that is to say, in most cases, your home-made annoyances, remembering that you are a Christian and not, as Madame de Sévigné used to say, *une jolie payenne*. You will soon understand why Descartes made his discoveries lying in bed through the mornings.

How can we secure solitude when our path is beset with a variety of undesirables? There is no answer to this question if we do not really crave solitude. But if we do, solitude will come, for no magnetism is as strong as a man's wish to be let alone. The day you will notice with satisfaction that you are glad of being kept waiting because

this gives you a chance of being left alone, you will know
that you really love solitude, and you will not have to
seek it or pray for it any more. Solitude will be where
you are. I know, in busy New York, a woman with a
home and family who manages to be five hours in an
upper room every morning, writing; I know another who
has rented a mysterious room on the ground-floor of her
own building and has never been found out yet, even by
her own maids. But I know another, apparently the very
type of the social woman with the most engaging smile on
her face; she is always in her house and never denies her
door, yet she reads serious literature, ancient and modern,
as if she had an ocean of leisure, and in fact never com-
plains of not having time enough. How can that be when
her telephone ought to be buzzing all the time? People are
afraid of this woman's wish to be let alone with her serious
books. They simply do not dare to ring up that number.

b) INTERIOR SOLITUDE

We call it concentration. As exterior solitude is the re-
duction of human beings and even of objects around us
to a minimum, concentration is the elimination, one after
the other, or by one sweeping effort, of all images foreign
to a train of thought. This train of thought is often spontaneous: we then call it absorption. Common parlance
rightly unites all mental conditions of this kind under the
term "to think." As long as whirlpools of uncontrolled
images fill our brain we are not supposed to think. The
moment images of the same nature come under our observation we know we think and simultaneously we become unconscious of most things extraneous to our
thought.

Who has not seen a man walking through a crowd
indifferent to all except his interior vision? George Tyrrell

had to be watched if one wished to keep him within the visible circle in which he was sitting: leave him two minutes to himself and he would be miles away. Lovers, poets, artists can thus be solitary in spite of their company. Alphonse Daudet never denied his door to any visitor. Only the caller, no matter who he was, was immediately given full details about the chapter on which the novelist was at work. Daudet's mind was apparently more active when he could speak his thoughts, and his invention was helped rather than hampered by the presence of his fellow-men. People dominated by one great passion, apostles of all degrees, live in their mastering purpose and do not need exterior solitude to think. It is difficult not to be struck by the contrast between Saint Paul's itinerant career and the concentration and condensation of his writings. We know he dictated his letters in rhythmical sentences. The presence of the secretary or interpreter did not disturb him; he was used to constant company and no doubt craved it. During the war a strange-looking person one day sat down next to me on a bench on the Terrace of Saint-German. He was a Russian workman, a simple man with just a few hundred words to his French vocabulary. In spite of this deficiency this man was eloquent. For more than an hour he poured himself out in a defense of pacifism which was not in season but which compelled my admiration all the same. Visibly my presence was only a pretext or an incentive for this worshipper of an absorbing idea.

Many people are professionally trained to concentration. Napoleon could pass from one subject to a completely different one, from strategy, for instance, to the Charter of the Comédie-Française, as if he had been another man. He had in his mind what he called sometimes drawers, sometimes atlases, providing him with the matter he required. Lawyers, or spiritual directors, often surprise us by the undivided attention they can give to one consultant after another, but they limit themselves to kindred cases and are collected rather than concentrated. However they too manage to live in an interior solitude which constant knocking at their door does not succeed in breaking. No doubt, such men are nearer to thought than the ordinary mortal, as a librarian is nearer to books than the costermonger in the street.

No complaint is more frequently heard than "I cannot concentrate" unless it be the other groan "I have no memory." On cross-examination you find that people who cannot concentrate are conscious either of a heaviness nullifying every intellectual effort, or of a volatility precluding any but a tip-of-the-wing contact with the object of attention. The moment they try to collect and focus their consciousness it seems as if there arose a whole flight of irrelevant images to mock and confuse them. If they fight this confusion nervousness frequently sets in, and its victim will in every case prefer frivolity to pain. This accounts for the numerous cases in which people are visibly trying to do anything rather than think. I have observed boys fidgeting and evidently ill at ease when an interesting book was read to the class. On the contrary, they would sit apparently contented when the tedious everyday drudgery went on. They hated the book, interesting enough to keep them from thinking of something else, but did not mind or rather liked the humdrum routine with its minimum demand and the freedom it left to their imagination.

Can we learn to concentrate? The doubt implied in this question is in itself an inferiority complex responsible for many a failure. As a matter of fact nine out of ten men or women who possess the capacity of folding their wings round their attention have acquired it by patient practice. The nature of our mind is, as has been shown in the first

part of this book, to superimpose sets of images; to eliminate as many of them as possible is an effort which only
necessity or some yearning can make a success. Attention
is less a gift than a habit, and the knowledge of this
ought to encourage those who wish to live inside their
own souls.

Nervousness is of course a tremendous obstacle to concentration. People who are made nervous by company,
who feel exaggeratedly the superiority in wit or looks of
others, who are made uncomfortable by tricks or affecta-
tions, ought not to blame themselves for feeling unable to
concentrate in the presence of their fellow-beings. Goldsmith certainly wrote like an angel: nothing can be more
logical, in spite of its gracefulness, than *The Vicar of
Wakefield*. When Oliver talked like poor Poll it was because he was made unbearably nervous and had to say
anything rather than endure the pressure. He was not talking like poor Poll the day he stopped some other writer's
praise with the admission that it tortured him to hear it.
Goldsmith ought to have avoided commune with literary
people who carry irritability everywhere with them. If you
are conscious of the same fluttering, seek kind, simple people rather than brilliant ones. When you are accosted by
someone whose talk you know by experience disturbs all
your concentration, smile, feel charitable and Christian,
but say nothing, keep immovably silent, till the other man's
sinister magnetism has spent itself in talk. You will be
aware of the moment when your chances become even
with his.

Interest of any kind produces concentration naturally.
Selfish people concentrate on their own immediate profits,
idealists on their idea. We cannot be five minutes with a
person without realizing what the nature and elevation of
his interest may be: whether it is gain, vanity or pleasure,
or whether it is some aspect of our multiform wish for the

world's betterment. Disinterestedness is its own reward, for it fills the soul more than any conscious effort. Nobility of point of view or purpose, an indifference to petty advantages, the charity of the true Christian, the never-interrupted contemplation of the mystic, all seem to us at the same time to confer intellectual superiority and to create a paradise for their possessor.

If we descend to the merely intellectual level, we shall find that here too real interest is essential for concentration and creates it in an instant. The same boy who goes wool-gathering when he has to write a literary essay can concentrate for half a day on mathematics or on a new radio implement. The same people who think they can only read the lightest kind of fiction can get pleasure out of innumerable memoirs undoubtedly easier to read than novels. They never dare to say that they concentrate on novels, because people would think it ridiculous, but they would not hesitate to admit that they concentrated on the *chroniques* of courts, and, in fact, they would know concentration as well as most historians. "Walk a hundred steps straight away from the main road"—Doudan says—"if you stick to one direction you will find some deliciously shaded spot or even a springing well." I used to know a French priest who, strangely enough, cared only for the theatre, a taste he could hardly indulge in a sleepy cathedral town. Beginning with the plays published by *L'Illustration,* this frivolous ecclesiastic gradually formed a vast dramatic collection. In a few years he was regarded as an authority on the modern drama, and when death interrupted an occupation which had become a specialty without ceasing to be a pleasure the sale of those volumes accumulated to satisfy a whim, was a literary event. To collect is to specialize and specialization is only another word for concentration. The upshot is that we are sure to concentrate the moment we have an interest or find a pleasure in doing so. The Art of Thinking is largely the finding out what gives our intellect its satisfaction without any effort or any restlessness.

However, we cannot always follow our inclination in thinking as we do in acting. There are dull problems that we have to tackle; we know intellectual duties not any easier to discharge than moral obligations: we may love poetry and dislike history, like Shelley, but we feel we must not imitate Shelley in his indifference to history, for only genius can disregard the general canons of culture. How can we concentrate on subjects which, not being attractive, naturally produce absent-mindedness? Another chapter will be devoted to mental exercises every one of which tends to create concentration. So would newspaper problems, questions and answers of all descriptions, cross word puzzles, etc. Madame de Maintenon, in her direct honest way, describes reflection as "thinking attentively several times over of the same thing." This definition provides excellent guidance when the object of our concentration is one and not many and when it lies well in the field of our mental microscope. But frequently things are complicated instead of being simple, or we are trying to discover—not just examine—thoughts, and the problem of concentration in such cases becomes different from mere attention to a schoolboy's lesson.

Let it be understood, to begin with, that concentration is impossible if we are fagged or dull. Too much sleep or too little sleep leaves a vacuum in our brain. So does too much eating or too much fasting. So does too much exercise or too little. Do not imagine that when you feel sleepy mentally, violent physical exercise, like squash, will wake you up. It will set all your animal spirits in motion, but tingling arteries generally go along with a spangly rush of disorderly images to the brain. Reading will not help your mind into what you think is the proper path either. Complete immobility, or a peaceful cigarette, or ten minutes at the open window, or strolling alone under the trees, or, sometimes, a cup of tea, will bring you nearer to the legitimate fountain of your thoughts than anything else.

When your heart is calmed by the unusual stillness of your mind, when the moths of distraction have dispersed, you are ready for concentration, but you may still find yourself facing a blank. Many intellectual workers are conscious that their effort to eliminate superfluity seems to have eliminated essentials as well. What do I want to think about? they wonder. What am I interested in? Am I interested in anything?

People endowed with good memories seldom experience this barrenness. On the least provocation their drawers or atlases fly open and they feel flush with data. It is the curse of most people so gifted that their data have long been stereotyped, borrowed as they often are from somebody else and never improved upon. On the contrary, people conscious of working on living matter, impressions, intuitions, or sentiments, pretty well pleased with their minds one day, disgusted the next, are, so to speak, cohabiting with nature, and their intellectual existence is a drama. Their very lack of memory makes them feel the necessity of continuity. They strive to rejoin themselves, to be in the natural flux of their conscious or sub-conscious existence from the days of childhood till now. Their memory is not an idelible board, it is more the consciousness of a few highlights, peaks of interest round which subordinate data naturally group themselves. Historians like Michelet or Carlyle obviously have memories organized in that way, but the main lines of even books like Gibbon's *Roman Empire*, or Fustel de Coulanges's *La Cité Antique*, show a dominant interest more purely intellectual, it is true, but still productive of crystallization. On the contrary, Mommsen—to whom I owe too much to speak of him disrespectfully—had an infallible but inorganic memory. Our effort ought to be to resume where we left off the last time we were vitally and completely active. We should never take up the newspaper without remembering that our interest in politics, that is to say, in contemporary history, must not be mere curiosity. We want the world to be wiser and less cruel; and, if there is a man or a country giving us hopes of the improvement foreseen by the Isaiahs of all countries, it is the progress of that man or that country that we want to follow. Our continuity on that plane is the condition of our memory as well as the channel of our concentration.

Concentration which, at first sight, is obtained by elimination, the elimination of images not harmonious with our trend of thought, can best be obtained by the conjuring of a suitable background. And this background is nothing else than the multiplication of harmonious images. If I want to concentrate, in order to understand it, on American isolation, for instance, I must, first of all, empty my sensibility of all irritation caused by narrow-minded defenses of this isolation, then I must rapidly people my imagination with such notions as the vastness of America —best realized by the extent of its lakes or its deserts, its lack of obtrusive neighbors, its self-supporting capacity, its tendency to conformity and its surprising realization of the words "foreign" and "foreigner"; I can remember that the Roumanian taxi-driver who once took me about in New York spoke to me of his country, left twenty years before, as if he had exchanged purgatory for Heaven; he helped me to understand the Pilgrims, men who had shaken the dust off their feet on the old continent—the very reverse of colonists; and the Pilgrims, in their turn, help me to understand the rebellious, the de-

fiant ring of the word "American" in the newspapers of
the pre-revolutionary period I have on a few occasions
consulted. It is enough. If I finally remember that Europe
appears to the untraveled American as a many-mouthed
hungry monster, my concentration is complete. I think
of nothing but the isolation of America and I understand
it so well that, were it not for another set of images near
by, I should promptly share in it. Multiply such visions
and distraction will not know where to have you.

This is the natural and vital way of thinking. All our
notions come from such groups of images and when we
wish to restore life to an idea hardening into words we
instinctively recall the concrete circumstances from which
it was originally evolved. Not otherwise do speakers who
hate memorising create in themselves the mood—both intellectual and imaginative—from which real eloquence
will flow. The interior cinema unrolling its pictures for
their benefit is not, like more abstract trains of thought, at
the mercy of distractions; and the hubbub of the dinner-
table, or the revolving scenery outside the carriage-win-
dow, hardly interferes with it.

Another infallible method of concentrating or, so to
speak, tempering one's attention, is to take pen in hand
and prepare to write down what our mind will dictate.
There is in the very gesture something imperative which
the most wandering mind seldom resists. A successful writer
whom I was asking about her methods of working told
me: "I take a blank sheet and a pencil, I sit at a perfectly bare table and pretty quickly a story comes." So
also did Anton Chekhov who wrote for the magazines
stories which were not magazine-stories like those of this
lady. But it is especially when we want to be clear and
definite, to make up our minds about some issue, that the
sheet and pencil process proves helpful.

Apart from the thing in which we are vitally interested,

the more or less conscious objects on which our egotism concentrates without any outward incentive, teacher, or advice, we spend our lives in vagueness. Most men and women die vague about life and death, religion or morals, politics or art. Even about purely practical issues we are far from being clear. We imagine that other people know definitely their own minds about their children's education, about their own careers, or about the use they should make of their money. The notion helps us to imagine that we ourselves are only separated from decision on these important issues by the lightest curtain of uncertainty. But it is not so. Other people, like ourselves, live in perpetual vagueness. Like us they foolishly imagine they are thinking of some important subject when they are merely thinking of thinking about it. When this fallacy has been nursed for some time in our subconsciousness we decide that the question admits of no compelling answer and we act according to the pressure of circumstances, or perfunctory advice, or the slogans of the moment. It is surprising how few people's testaments are really their wills. They had never been able to know their own minds, so the lawyer or some relation dictated the document.

If we should sit before the blank sheet, and write on two columns the arguments pro and con an idea that occurs to us, the truth would flash on us. We should either be struck by the evidence of some considerations or, no less startlingly, should we see the necessity for seeking advice on this or that point. Advice of whom? Do not go back to the illusion of just thinking of thinking about the possible persons. Take another sheet and write down the *pros* and *cons* concerning advisers. Quite instinctively you will keep those sheets in one envelope. This will be a *dossier,* in every point similar to those shaping the destinies of empires.

Robinson Crusoe had recourse to this method when he

could have recourse to nothing else. Saint Ignatius Loyola describes it at full length and has made it the basis of spiritual life in his Society; few people know that the fifty odd folio diaries left by that incomparable adviser, Prince Albert, hold the written preparation of the suggestions he used to give Queen Victoria. Try the system once, you will never desert it. It is only fair to warn you that the habit is apt to become tyrannical; you will mechanically reach for your pad and pencil not only when you have to decide about selling your house, but even when you have to pack up a trunk. Everything has its inconveniences and I will point out more fully further down some drawbacks of fixing one's thought by writing. But making up our mind is a necessity and better be an unsuspected crank than too visible a weathercock.

On the whole, concentration is a natural state which can easily be reproduced by simple methods. It is only supposed to be exceptional because people do not try and, in this, as in so many other things, starve within an inch of plenty. Those who do try have never been disappointed in the process but have sometimes experienced disappointment in themselves.

"I only find ordinary thoughts," they complain.

"Yes, but they are your own and better produce ordinary thoughts than nothing."

"I do see glimpses of deep truth or am conscious of brilliant flashes, but they vanish like will o' the wisps."

"Blessed are you. You will not be eloquent, but you will be phosphorescent."

A few years ago I sat at dinner next to an American woman who charmed me by the subtlety of her judgment, but whose short flights constantly disappointed expectations constantly rising again. Yet, I never can open Joubert without thinking of her, a great achievement for a society woman. And did not Montaigne admit, without much concern, that he could "charge a difficulty only once or twice after which he had to look away from it"? Boys who try to read the hour on a church-clock a mile off know the dodge. What we are expected to do is only to make the most of our possibilities.

c) MAKING TIME

Have you really no time? Are you sincere, or are you just repeating what everybody else is saying? No time! The extremity of poverty! Perhaps your idea of having time is not having *some* time to yourself, but having *all* the time, having nothing to do: Examine your conscience and answer.

Axiom: Very busy people always find time for everything.

Conversely, people with immense leisure find time for nothing.

Perhaps you do not know what concentration means. If so, sell all your possessions, leave your dearest and nearest, and having re-read the previous chapter devote three days or maybe three hours to exercises in concentration. You will soon find out whether you know how to concentrate or not.

In the meantime, you will do well to ask yourself a few questions.

1—About saving time.

Is there no time you can reclaim, not from your work, not from your exercise, not from your family or friends, but from pleasure that really does not give you much pleasure, from empty talk at the Club, from inferior plays, from doubtfully enjoyable week ends or not very profitable trips?

Have you learned how not to give in to idlers? Can you

steel yourself against the temptation to give pleasure to people whose laziness needs no assistance? Do you discriminate between kindness and weakness, never refusing to do a good turn, but always refusing to be a dupe? Are you an absolute slave to the telephone?

Do you know how to gather up fragments of time lest they perish? Do you realize the value of minutes? One of the Lamoignons had a wife who always kept him waiting a few minutes before dinner which in those days was in broad daylight, at three o'clock. After a time it occurred to him that eight or ten lines could be written during this interval, and he had paper and ink laid in a convenient place for that purpose. In time—for years are short but minutes are long—several volumes of spiritual meditations were the result. Mankind might be divided between the multitude who hate to be kept waiting because they get bored and the happy few who rather like it because it gives them time for thought. The latter lead the rest, of course.

What do you do in trains, cars or taxis? If you do nothing in perfect contentment, well and good, but if you feel restless you are to blame. Trollope, who was a commuter, wrote many a chapter in the train. You might read these: they are worth your while, and Trollope is in fashion. You cannot be reading or thinking without avoiding company: people no doubt will remark that Vere de Vere keeps much to himself, but it cannot be helped. If you try to think, you must expect to be a little apart and not a little above.

Do you carry a little book, a great little book of the approved President Eliot description, or, oh joy! one of your own finding, in your breast pocket?—"It isn't done" —"Oh! I beg your pardon, I meant a pack of cards of course. Excuse my absent-mindedness."

What time do you get up? Could it not be three quarters of an hour, or half an hour earlier? If you give up reading in bed—a practice condemned by all oculists and by not a few moralists, you can manage it. Nobody has ever been able to explain why a Latin education should give that curious superiority to people, but it does. There is the same mystery about saving the morning—"Clean up the morning trench," Fénelon wrote to a lady—"for intellectual work." Somehow it does the trick. An hour in the morning is worth two, and the nothingness that must inevitably come in the silly hours afterwards will not submerge you.

2—*About frittering time away*

Do you often hear yourself saying: "I forgot" or "I didn't think"? These ejaculations mean that you are losing time, have to go over beaten ground several times, through your own fault. We should never forget, at all events so seldom that it will be a surprise.

You will hardly ever forget, you will not be fumbling and recommencing, if you possess two easily acquired habits, foresight and order. To foresee means to imagine in advance. A quarter of an hour can easily be saved in the Pullman if you have visualized what night or morning things ought to be on the top of your suit-case instead of lurking where the fingers will anxiously feel for them with an accompanying scowl of the brow. Foresee that the customs examination means your trunk-key in a well-defined pocket. If you are liable to the emigration man's cross-examination, do not trust to your passport alone, but have in readiness a letter, asked in advance of your American hostess, where there will be references to Long Island week-ends or to the Opera, but no references to lecturing, for lecturing is sure to mean atheism or Bolshevism. If you forget to write for that letter four weeks before sailing it will come after you have sailed. If you forget it in your stateroom and have to fetch it therefrom amid the disgust and scorn of the other aliens, you will find that your trunk has just been moved out of your cabin and is somewhere on its way to letter D.

These are elementary exercises in imaginative foresight. You will do well to visualize more important possibilities such as marriage, old age, illness, death or lunacy, failure in this or incomplete success in that, errors on your part and treason or stupidity on the part of others. Read the future, do not be the bleating sheep or the silly frisking lamb, and as your imagination shows you things as they will probably be, only not so bad, jot them down and keep the notes carefully. With surprising rapidity you will find yourself in the possession of notebooks telling you with fulness and clarity all you must do preparatory to moving out or selling out or other important outs and ins.

"What a bore!" you exclaim, "what a slavery to things!"—No! what freedom! what independence and security! My note-book is a fortune. So is another fat dossier in which my blunders are recorded for profitable private reading.

Order is the sister of foresight, as you can see. He is unnatural who, visualizing a call on So and So does not put in his greatcoat pocket, or next to his hat, the book long ago borrowed of So and So. A bench in the hall strewn with things that have to go out, memos on the rug round your desk do not mean untidiness but order. Things should be where they will not be forgotten.

"Are you sure you know the difference between order and tidiness, dear Madam? Your boudoir certainly looks wonderfully well-groomed and manicured, but where is that rather important letter which came Saturday from the lawyer?" Ah! where is it? If we should peep under the cover of that exquisite *bonheur du jour* what should we

see? What a conglomeration of letters, some in their envelopes, some out of them, of bills, of invitations, concert
tickets, old programs and what not! How long it will take
to find the lawyer's letter! How many times will the
dainty fingers dart at a pile of papers, in the firm belief
that the note must be there, only to get out of it with
the impatience of the disappointed humming-bird!

Now let us go at it with a little order. Let us have on
this chair the opened letters, on that table the others, on
the *Standard Dictionary* the bills, everything else in the
waste basket.

"Wait! on one of those programs, oh! on one of those
programs are two lines of Crashaw which I would not lose
for the world."

"Here they are. Where do they go?"

"Ah! where? In the *Cambridge History of Literature,*
section Crashaw? . . ."

"No, believe me, fetch a large strong envelope, tear it
open at the top, write Crashaw on it, put in that program,
and lay it on one of your shelves. Pretty soon there will
be fifty more such wrappers and your husband will say
admiringly that this is a regular office. . . . Now, glance
at the opened letters. Not a red pencil mark on any,
you surprise me. Well, you have to read the letters all over
again. . . . All these useless? Why are they kept then?
Tear them to pieces and into the waste basket."

"These two from Mrs. Chambers I want to keep."

"Big envelope, Chambers written on top, lay next to
Crashaw. Simplify."

"These two, these four, these fifteen have to be answered."

"Heavens! I understand why all foreigners complain
that Americans do not answer letters. Most business-like
nation in the world; Well, there is no help for it. You
are a lady, you must answer letters. Take fifteen envelopes,

put the fifteen letters in them and, in the bitterness of your heart, write fifteen superscriptions. Henceforth, the moment a letter comes, you will red-pencil the important passages, ask yourself whether this letter is for the waste basket, the Chambers-Crashaw shelf, or the to-be-answered pile. If the latter, put the letter in an envelope, write the superscription, affix stamp—if the letter goes to Paris, please, do please stamp with a five and not with a two, as you always do—the higher this pile of unanswered letters rises the worse your conscience will feel, and annoyance will teach you virtue.

"Why! There's the *bonheur du jour* empty! and here's the waste basket full! and here's a happy surprised smile on your face, and you know now the difference between tidiness which is hypocrisy and order which means a place for everything and everything in its place, whether it be a shelf, an envelope, or the waste basket.

"Do not say that it only took half an hour to clean out the little desk and consequently you only wasted thirty minutes by not being methodical. For the same jumble that was in your desk was also in your mind, and even in your life, my dear lady; you lost time and thought little of it, but moreover you were ineffective, a poor fumbling tennis player who never gave a smash. Your ideal should be never to waste a step, a word or a gesture. Looseness is the reverse of elegance. Indeed it is in everything the first cousin of slovenliness."

Next to lack of order, one of the most fatal ways of wasting time as well as weakening one's life is to hesitate before acting. A friend of mine came back from his four years in a prisoners' camp in Germany with the nervous inability to decide called *abulia*. I was watching him one day when he stood before the hat rack for a full minute uncertain on which peg he should hang his *képi*. The scene was pathetic. It is only irritating when the hesitancy is the consequence, not of ill health, but of lack of energy, intelligence, or method. Some people can dress in forty minutes, because they have learned the automatism which M. Bergson used to recommend so persuasively. Others will take an hour and a half either because they have not adopted the invariable order which, in time, becomes automatism, or because they hesitate before decisions which ought to be mere gestures. You see them looking round and wondering what next, sometimes looking out at the window or smoking a cigarette to brighten up their wits, or endlessly hesitating between two collars or two ties.

An old French word preserved only in a few Northern districts describes this graphically. It is the verb *tourniquer* which shows us a person aimlessly moving in a circle till an inspiration for definite action comes. Of course the circling has a tendency to last longer while the inspiration grows slower. Some people simply use up their lives thus beginning and not beginning to begin. Five minutes before a sheet of paper with the famous question of Foch on top: *De quoi s'agit-il?"* and a pencil to answer it, would break the sinister charm, but chronic hesitancy looks for no remedy. Its answer to itself is: we must first think about it; but the thinking never begins. In fact the word beginning is terrifying. Nothing can be truer and more encouraging to men equally gifted with a human desire for action and a human indulgence of laziness than the Greek sentence: *The beginning is half the thing.* Writers know it well. Students at school ought to be taught how true it is. You have to write at college an essay on Ronsard. Go straight to the French professor who can best give you a list of a dozen passages showing you Ronsard at his most sublime, at his most graceful, at his worst greco-latin, etc. Go straight home and read these, making notes of what you observe and of how you react. Lose no time and sort these notes. Think about them till some flesh comes on these bones, and, without losing time, write down what you have to say and say no more.

Your will can be prepared and drawn up in the same way. So can your answer to a proposal for a partnership. So can your Machiavellian campaign for bringing So and So round to offering you a partnership. Learn to attack things frontally but according to the most scientific methods. Be the Lindbergh of whatever little ocean you have to cross. Our life should consist of a thousand brief dramas, complete in themselves, swift as a game of poker. Some business men have given me a truly artistic pleasure by the infallibility of their dictation. Each letter meant a rapid weighing of *pros* and *cons*, a decision, and the thing done at once. Other business men. . . .

Have you ever begun to learn French or German? Yes? and you feel like beginning again? Believe me, do not. One experiment should be enough. The demon of hesitancy delights in telling people that they ought to learn languages. Rather collect match-boxes like the Russian prince in *Sylvestre Bonnard*. He had only one missing specimen to find and the search filled his life. Much rather begin today, this very morning, some kind of social work that will give you a right to eat your dinner without shame.

So time can be "made" and the well-worn phrase is not a deception. If you possess lists of things to be done in given circumstances (before going to the country, before sailing, before entering on a study) ; if your agenda is a clearly-sectioned table showing you at a glance what you have to do, you will be a busy person, but you will have a sense of power over things. And if you know how to concentrate, i. e., how to use the keen edge of your mind, having time and possessing the tool, you will only need good material for thought. It is to this material that the next chapters will be devoted.

Chapter Eight

LIVING ONE'S LIFE ON A HIGHER PLANE

a) THOUGHT-PRODUCING IMAGES

Remember that our mind is active on a constant succession of more or less connected images. These images, as we said, characterize our mental quality. Pass from a noble art gallery to the picture department of a store, and you will be conscious of mediocrity coming after distinction. Every man's imagination is a picture gallery. If the pictures were visible, instead of having to be inferred from the talk or general deportment of the individual, we could grade our fellow-beings as we do vases in a shop.

It is useless to do more than recall what was said in §2 of Part I about the general inferiority of the images filling the minds of most human beings. Many of them are hardly superior to those constituting the mentality of the animal, always remembering that animals are not infrequently far above human beings in sensibility or in the capacity for love. The mind of an habitual drunkard, or that of an undeveloped peasant, knows little besides images connected with elemental wants. Sex maniacs, of whom there are more than people imagine, even the average specimen, the well-dressed man who follows women through the streets, are almost incapable of producing more than one category of images. Misers, men who build a fortune, as modern parlance prefers to say, are also hypnotized by one tyrannical set of pictures. So is the ambitious worldling, the social climber who sees on his inward scroll mostly press notices of his attendance at committees and public banquets or decorations and titles. The most usual type, of course, is the man or woman imprisoned in his or her paltry existence, and endlessly attentive to its shabby details. Jane Austen is almost ferocious in her descriptions of the superior specimens of this inferior type, the one of course which we jostle every day.

We all probably have a word in our vocabulary to describe this all-pervading mediocrity. When I was a boy in our little French town I used to patronize a shop kept by a M. Pailla who was also something of a farmer and was not devoid of the something that makes a gentleman. He was a rotund and short elderly chap unexpectedly nimble on his little feet. While looking round his shop for the particular bonbons or jujubes I wanted, he would lend an ear to the conversation kept up by his tall wife and lean daughters in the next room. I came away disappointed when I did not hear him sputter out his disgusted appreciation of their tattle: " '*tits détails, 'tits détails!*'" which stood for *petits détails*, and has served me through life to characterize inwardly nineteen-twentieths of what I hear and not a little of what I say.

Can we think as we like? or is not our thought as fated as our breathing?

Certainly we cannot help thinking any more than we can help breathing, but, just as we can choose to breathe pure air in a pine wood on a high hill, we can place our mind where the images it will work upon will be of a higher nature. What is to prevent me from replacing the gossip of Main Street by the gossip of Europe? Nobody can take real interest in the affairs of the world without conferring a living personality on those great *dramatis personae* of history: the old nations of Europe, the strange resurgent peoples of Asia, or America now fully come of age. I can speak of Great Britain and the United States as I might of two of my neighbors. It will take a great deal of observation of the latter to give a broad human value to what I may say of them, but if I say of Britain that a long habit of world-wide power has prepared her *élite* for shouldering responsibilities, whereas America, not quite conscious yet of her new power, is more willing to be kind than to be a leader, I shall be expressing a thought. Such is the influence of a vast scene as compared with a narrow one.

In the same way Signor Mussolini was personally as interesting or even more so twenty years ago than now, yet what we learn about him day after day is history and not personality.

Again, there is but little difference between the interests, ambitions and rivalries of nations and those of clans or families, as young students of history ought to be told from the beginning, yet, international questions seem to belong to only a few privileged observers.

Nothing can be farther away from the truth. Neither Madame de Sévigné, nor Saint-Simon, nor most authors of memoirs possessed a wide range of political judgment, but they now seem high above their fellows because their interest was of a dignified order. Anybody can rise to that level and must blame himself if he does not. During the war millions of simple individuals did it without the least affectation and yet in the proper tone, because the daily topic was history. Today they have relapsed to mere stories and their thinking has lost proportionately. Yet, the same elements for high and wide thinking daily offer themselves. I have never forgotten the sunny Sunday in 1914 when the extras announcing the Sarajevo news were sold on the boulevards. I could overhear a few people talking history, but most looked away from this tragic overture of the greatest drama in history to go back to the winner at Longchamps, for it was the day of the Grand Prix. Hardly a week passes, during the history-fraught years we are living, without such a chance for natural yet high speculation coming our way. Still, most people insist on talking about Jones or Brown.

It is strange that so many professional critics should make the mistake of seeking original subjects among the lesser characters in literary history. Some minors, of course, are of paramount interest to the historian because, clumsily or unwittingly, they started an important movement. Arthur Young counts in the history of Romanticism, and Champfleury means more than Flaubert in the apparition of Realism, but one book about Young or Champfleury is enough, whereas libraries can be written about Balzac, Flaubert or Byron. If a young scholar asks me for a subject about which plenty can be said that has never as yet been said, I reply unhesitatingly: Homer, Plato, Virgil, Milton, Racine, or Alexander, Caesar, Napoleon, or the Apostolic Age, or the Revolution, or Death, or Love. The test should be: what is likely to interest an intelligent child? for children do not care for trivial details till they have been spoiled by imitation. As for the *a posteriori* proof, it is plentiful. What book on Napoleon has *not* been successful? Would a young woman like Madame de Staël have made her mark, as she did, had not her high intellect been attracted, from the first, by such vital subjects as the human passions, the foundations of literature, the Revolution, or German Romanticism? What parts of such an all-embracing production as Sainte-Beuve's do we re-read, and which do we skip? Do we ever prefer a collection of match-boxes to one of Raphaels? The curse of daily journalism is that the triviality of its topics invites perfunctoriness in treatment. The moment the headline takes us back to something rich and deep, the reporter makes room for a poet.

It is impossible to spend an hour in a room with a man approaching greatness without feeling the contagiousness of distinguished thinking. Such men cannot always be found, or our chances for meeting them may be limited. But anybody with an average knowledge of the history of nations, literature, philanthropy, or art, not to speak of the history of great religionists or saints, can people his imagination with groups of superior men in every realm. I shall have an occasion further on to point out how we can summon any great man to bear us company when we feel at all lonely, but our serious hours cannot be devoted to a more useful occupation than studying the lives or ideas of great men.

Plutarch's *Parallel Lives* gave first-rate food to the minds of the *élite* in all nations until it was regarded as a classic instead of an amusing book. Madame de Maintenon, who was neither a king's mistress, as too many people in America curiously believe, or a bore, as modern French people foolishly imagine, tells us that her Huguenot mother insisted on her and her brother constantly bringing Plutarch's heroes into their games as well as conversations, and adds that the command was obeyed with delight. The French school-boy does not read any more Plutarch than his syllabus compels him to wade through for his Greek examination, but he replaces him by his textbook on French literature: children love the exceptional and abhor banality in other people's as well as in their own lives. Musset's moral example is a poor substitute for Demosthenes; but as Musset's weaknesses finally produced the poetry of the *Nuit d'Octobre,* the boyish inference is that there is an elegant way of being ordinary and that is what should be copied. His mind is full of this thought when you discover an unwonted gravity on his brow while he packs his books into his *serviette.* Who can say that this boy's thought is not nearer to real thinking than it will be ten years later when the smart young lawyer or financier will be attentive mostly to money, success, and women?

No remedy for the banality of thought produced by the inferiority of our lusts can equal the meditation of great lives. Open Clemenceau's little book on Demosthenes and you will see and positively touch as with your own hand the effect of a constant preference for great patriots and great thinkers in an existence which journalism, politics, duelling and all the empty effervescence of the Forum might otherwise have made shallow. Many degrees below Clemenceau I have more than once seen Socialist ranters rise to unexpected dignity by merely claiming that their action is in a line with that of the great Revolutionists. The sole mention of greatness acts magically because we all realize its unfailing influence upon us.

If, at any moment, you are unable to name a great man who is, or has recently been, having an influence on your conduct, you will be passing the verdict: ORDINARY on the quality of your own thought and existence. Conversely, give me the public utterances of this or that politician or so-called leader, and I shall be able to tell you whether he is haunted by some irresistible souvenir of greatness or merely moved by the interests in the air. America does not realize how much she owes to the fact that Lincoln is still a living presence on the Capitol hill, unavoidable even if it is not sought.

Unconvinced? cold? miles away from Lincoln or Plutarch, my fair young reader? *Ah! que la vie est quotidienne!* Still you need not despair and commit suicide by plunging headlong into chocolates or boys. Surely you like nature. I met you once alone and happy on the cliff-way in Newport. You like music, you like pictures, and you adore laces. The idea of Rome means something to you when you cross the gangway to the *Duilio*. It is enough. What a distinguished person you would be, what a brilliant parterre your mind would look like if you would generally exclude that which does not give you the greatest en-

joyment of which you are capable. But it is one of the
mysteries of our nature that when our table is laden with
delicious things, we go and cry before Mother Hubbard's
cupboard.

b) MORAL ELEVATION A CONDITION OF HIGH THINKING

"Great thoughts arise from the heart" Vauvenargues
says; and Joubert: "There is no light in souls in which
there is no warmth."

The modern French, in spite of Romanticism, show a
growing tendency to rejoin the Greeks in their purely intellectual view of the production of thought. Yet, they will
not infrequently belie their philosophy by utterances like
the above. In fact, it is impossible to live without noticing
how barren our intellect becomes when it is supposed to
be given unbounded chances. On the other hand, we
must all meet some day with men intellectually our in-
feriors, yet for whose thoughts we cannot help expressing
admiration. Read the life of that French beggar, Saint
Labre, living in rags and filth on the steps of the Roman
churches. Read the life of the humble *curé* of Ars, Jean-
Baptiste Vianney, so little gifted intellectually that he was
all but refused for ordination at a period when the French
clergy was too depleted to be fastidious. These two men
knew nothing, but they saw everything, and their view of
the world, what they would have been surprised to hear
called their philosophy and its expression, were of supreme
distinction. Look at their pictures. You will see in their
eyes and over their faces something luminous which means
nothing if it does not reflect thought.

Love, whether it be the attraction of Truth, or pure,
simple, elemental love, always opens up the intellect and
gives it the freedom of genius. Maternity also acts in that
way. Animals of course show it wonderfully, and—let it be

said without any attempt at cheap paradoxicalness—even artificial women show it too. The transformation lasts as long as the flow of love retains its power.

So does any great altruistic impulse filling the whole soul. The war gave a unique chance to thousands of men and women with unemployed reserves of devotion. I remember a well-known American woman who called on me at the Pavillon Belgiojoso, in the Collège Stanislas, towards 1908. She wanted information about the movement of the *Sillon,* at that time in its full force. But I felt that she would have welcomed information about anything that might have given her soul-energies a chance. I remember the eager questions in the throaty but distinguished voice: every word betrayed a suppressed longing for something that would liberate her head and heart. The war gave her the chance which her yearning was praying for. She spent herself freely and her reward came at once. I met her again in California in 1919. She had undergone a transformation similar to that which a happy marriage is often known to produce. The suppressed impassioned something which made her at the same time distinguished and pitiful had disappeared, but in its place there was a superb fulness in the working of the mind and a mastery of persuasive language. Fulfilment was implied in every nuance.

Her case is one of many thousands. A missionary of the real kind, a hospital worker of the real kind, the innumerable varieties of social workers, women of the type of Mrs. Howe, or Florence Nightingale, or Sister Rosalie, apparently merely devoted to an ideal of action, are transformed mentally by it, and, as Madame Guyon used to say, could write or speak endlessly about it. Intellectual inferiority complexes melt away like thin snow in the proximity of love, and the liberation of the soul is complete.

Nowhere is there such a chance of this liberation as in

the United States where the primitive impulse towards corporative and coöperative betterment, far from having spent itself, seems to be in full force. Whoever has been engaged, were it once in his life, in the instructive task of collecting money for a charity must have learned that, contrary to the general belief, many Americans of means can refuse a dollar, but also that nowhere will an idea worth collaboration find such collaborators as it finds there. Intellectual generosity—of which charity is only the natural sequence—is an instinct with the American. It is not surprising therefore that he should find so many chances of developing through pure love, and that the corporate thinking of the United States, what people call its ideal, should be of an exceptional quality.

But suppose these chances should fail honest desire, suppose all men were happy and fifty-six thousand stray cats had not been found enduring misery in the streets of Boston alone in one year, would it not yet be possible to rise up to the region of thought through moral efforts? Stop the stream of your consciousness for an instant, look into your soul, arrest the images forming and dissolving there. What will you see? Petty self-love, of course, but even more frequently, petty irritations. Our nature is neither noble nor generous. We remember slights more easily than kindnesses. We may have lived for days in a home or a foreign country without meeting with anything except courtesy. The moment we feel irritated or offended we forget the happiness and nurse the paltry grievances. We are touchy and on our guard. Self-seeking possesses us. As we get older and should be more detached we become on the contrary more alert to the main chance. A studied appearance of frankness which we acquire in the course of years veils realities which we would not care to exhibit for inspection. Joseph de Maistre once said he did not know what a scoundrel's soul might be, but he knew well what the soul of a good man consisted of, and it was horrid. It is the whispered confession of us all. No wonder therefore if, instead of noble images filling our minds, there should be there a plentiful crop not only of *'tits détails,* but of pretty low visions. Thought worth the name can never arise from a nasty growth. But just as we can prefer decent company to ordinary or worse, or good books to poor ones, we can crush out inferior thought, and invite better ones. Just as we learn to sit up straight, or do not give in, even in our privacy, to too much freedom of attitudes, we can drive out soul visitors we are not proud of. This humble beginning of sanctity will be rewarded by a straighter judgment and by that broader sympathy which is an aspect of intelligence. Good men generally think right. When they do not, it seems unnatural, and the lower parts of our soul, the insurgents in us always ready for an outcry, triumph meanly.

c) HIGHER THOUGHTS FROM BOOKS

If you will refer to § c. of Chapter 6, Part II, on the danger of weak reading, you will know what to expect from this. Reading, to most people, means an ashamed way of killing time disguised under a dignified name. Trifling with print in that manner quickly diminishes the resilience of the intellect. It goes directly against an Art of Thinking.

If you wish to use books as an adjunct to thought, they must be books that will not merely amuse or put your mind to sleep, but, on the contrary, will keep it wide awake and alert.

What are those books?

What they are *you* know best, and I do not know in the least. A book, like a landscape, is a state of consciousness varying with readers. There exists some book, pamphlet, article in an encyclopedia, or possibly an old clipping from a newspaper that once set you thinking; there may be many; indeed you may be one of those rare beings with whom a few lines of print are food enough for thought because, as Lamartine says, their thoughts think themselves. The something evocative for you may be poetry, history, philosophy, the sciences, or moral sciences, i. e., the progress of mankind. Some people who go to sleep over a volume will be interested by a review which they think more condensed or better within their reach. Read reviews if they help you to think, that is to say if they leave in your mind images that will go on living when you have forgotten where they came from; read a Shakespeare calendar at the rate of four lines a day, if Shakespeare quotations have on you the magic influence they have on some people; read algebra, read the lives of great inventors or of great businessmen, read *that* kind of books which you and nobody else know to be thought-productive for you.

Some people get more poetry out of ten lines of classical Thomson than out of the whole of Shelley because they first read those ten lines in childhood or in a peculiarly receptive mental condition. In the same way, there may be a deeper source of romanticism in the brave melancholy of a seventeenth century minuet, than in a Wagner opera. Nobody can think our thoughts for us, and nobody can tell us what will act as dew or sun on our thinking. The book that makes us think is the book we cannot shut again after we have read one page, because we are entranced by what it says to us; or it is the book we drop on our knee after reading one page, because what it says starts us irresistibly questioning, contradicting, or supplementing. No titles, no categories can be given to you by anybody but yourself, and what I am going to say hereafter should not intimidate you into doubting the wisdom of your answer to the entirely personal question: what books help me the best to think?

Sir Walter Scott thought out his novels while reading books perfectly foreign to his subject, and who can doubt but Kant was visited by philosophical inspirations while going through those narratives of travel he was so fond of? Have you ever analyzed what has been going on in your mind when you have been pleased with a lecture or a concert? Sometimes you may have enjoyed following the argument or the music with more than usual clarity; oftener the speech or the motif have given a chance to some lurking activity deep in you and, during an hour, you have been at your most personal. The Art of Thinking is merely the art of being that, as easily and as frequently as possible.

Never read a book for the style. Newman's biographies say that he used to read *Mansfield Park* every year for that, for the style. Newman, himself a master of infallible English, must have been sensible of the exquisite quality of Jane Austen's language, but he was too much above mere words or mere elegance to care for what people call the style of an author, that is to say the gestures of his expression. So ought we to be if we do not wish to fall to the level of the pedant dealing in mere words and whose masterpiece can only be a cento. A decided attitude in this respect will place us at once among the group of the virile people with whom the substance of things is all-important. What a man means, where it tends to, and what use it will be to us and to our fellow-beings is what we want to know. If the Christian habit of seeing everything *sub specie aeternitatis* raises this attitude to the finality and charity that cannot belong to the merely intellectual order, we shall be gainers.

And what books should we so read?

The principle which has never failed to confer superiority on a man's thinking activity is the well-worn precept: DO NOT READ GOOD BOOKS—life is too short for that—ONLY READ THE BEST. This simple recipe is as infallible as good air and good food are in physical hygiene. Yet, it is a fact that nineteen out of twenty modern people quake away from it. "Masterpieces again," they groan, "The *Aeneid,* the *Divina Commedia, Paradise Lost,* we have heard that before: much rather be ordinary than bored."

The notion that masterpieces are boresome school books interpreted by dull teachers, or examination stuff, is a marvellous product of education. Ignorance is assuredly less deadly, for it can create no such inferiority complex as the schoolboy's notion of his lack of kinship with the best literature. But this phantasm can easily be exorcised if we modify the above principle to: ONLY READ WHAT GIVES YOU THE GREATEST PLEASURE.

In the past century there lived in London a clerk of the retiring disposition behooving a man of little means, yet with a turn for the brilliant in civilization, especially for the theatre, for beautiful actresses, for talent and elegance. This man was a playgoer of course, but, in his leisure hours in the daytime, he would read plays, plays of all times and all countries, plays of any description, provided they gave him pleasure. No reader ever placed his own enjoyment more decidedly before any other consideration. We know his impressions, we can hardly be better informed about the mental background of anybody than about this absolute dilettante. Uniquely by his untiring application to pleasing himself and by his delight in analyzing his pleasure, this man achieved no mean originality. It is evident that, had he compelled himself to read famous sermons, as many of his contemporaries still did, he would have made his life not only less enjoyable but useless. His name was Charles Lamb. When we look into the

kind of literature he used to read, we discover it was the
pink of dramatic literature, and the prejudice against perfection left on us by the defects of teaching or teachers is
so strong that immediately our chin falls and we know
the familiar impression of disgust.

For all that, Lamb had a superb time all his life reading his sixteenth century dramatists, a much better time
than trash, unhampered by any inferiority complex, can
ever give even us.

A few years ago I travelled from Montreal down to
Boston in a Pullman car which, strange to say, never contained more than three passengers till we reached our
destination. Opposite me sat a McGill girl—a junior I
inferred from her conversation with two other girls who
were seeing her off. On the other side of the aisle sat a
young man, one of those handsome, perfectly well-tai-
lored American youths, so attractive that you are willing
to ascribe genius to them as well as a host of minor per-
fections. This demi-god was reading. The McGill girl
looked across at him for some time till their eyes met.
"Reading?" she half queried, after an interval of mute
presentation leading to a simultaneous smile. "Yes," a
very uncultivated voice answered, "what I want is a love
story with a kid in it and lots of deviltry in him." The
book was handed across the aisle and the girl began to
read. The voice had been an anti-climax and so, evidently, was the book, yet the girl read on, skimming
and skipping. After a while my professorial conscience
smote me and bending over the love-and-kid-story I
whispered: "Have you ever read *Vanity Fair?*" The girl
looked up, flushed a little and answered: "Dickens?"—
"No," I said, "Thack . . ."—"Oh! Thackeray, of course!
No, it was not on our list."

What would I not have given to have *Vanity Fair* in
my valise, open it at random and watch the girl's delight

at Becky Sharp's introduction to Sir Pitt's town-house and to his immortal charwoman!

"You have never read *Vanity Fair*, which is a wonderfully interesting book," I said, "and you waste an hour on a kid-and-love-story which bores you to death."

The girl certainly was bored to death but she was not convinced. As long as masterpieces appear as books "which are on our list," trash is sure to be preferred. Better be bored by it than excited by great books.

Assignments, examination papers and the commentaries of pedants are largely responsible for this. For, the moment a great book is not supposed to be one, it recovers at once its original value as entrancing reading. Another train incident once gave me a tangible proof of this fact. I was in the Paris to Orléans train. Opposite me an intelligent-looking but countrified man was sorting papers. In the corner, on my side of the compartment, his little daughter, a child of twelve in black, was reading a square little book also habited in black canvas by some amateur bookbinder. I never saw anybody read like that. It seemed as if the old-fashioned but pretty and dainty little figure were trying to lose itself in that book. In time my curiosity about a book that could be read with such intensity became irresistible. I made a brief feint of talking with the father and then suddenly turned to the little girl and asked: "What are you reading so delightedly?" The eager little face looked up, summoned, as it were, from faraway regions. *"Monsieur, c'est l'Histoire Romaine"* (brief pause) *"et je vais arriver à Jules César!"*—"How do you know you are coming to Julius Caesar?"—"Oh! I have read this book many times."

I have never forgotten the emphasis on: *"et je vais arriver à Jules César!"* No prospect of Christmas, graduation, first European trip, or *début*, ever produced emphasis of that quality. I visualized the background in an instant: a farm on the windy plain of wheatfields between long strips of grape vines, the *salle* with its big mantel-piece; on the side ledge of this, below the ancestral powder-horns, the tiny library of three or four musty pray-er-books, a gardening book, a cook-book, a surveyor's man-ual, a Family Lawyer, a Larousse *Dictionary,* a few old almanacs and, in the faraway corner, the little black can-vas *Histoire Romaine.* In a modern library of fiction or magazines the squat volume would have been as forbidding to a child as a black old monk. Next to the Lawyer's or Surveyor's stuff, Roman History resumed its glamour and Julius Caesar became once more the romantic hero he was during so many centuries. Owing to an incredible chance the little girl summed up in herself the dreams, yearnings and admirations of princesses. No wonder she looked distinguished.

This is what classics do when they are not killed by those who teach them, or, above all, when they are not juxtaposed with trash sure to make them look like the brown bread of Auvergne as compared to cheap sweets. None of the inferior stuff to which our children are treated, while we look on powerless, can ever give them the feeling of elation, nay, the amusement which great books naturally produce.

So, if you want to be vitalized into the power of think-ing real thoughts, and if you want never to know one dull instant while reading, do what has been done by the best specimens of mankind since there have been books, res-olutely leave out whatever is not of the best. If something in you rebels against this, you are not in the mood for reading this book, you care for no Art of Thinking, or you only want mental lozenges which I cannot produce, and so farewell. But let it not be till you have drawn up a list of the great books which do possess some attraction for you, and till a few months' experience has shown you

which of these gives you unmixed pleasure. Those twenty
or thirty volumes will be *your* library, that is to say, your
fountain of thought, your delight, and when you see people
envying you your pleasure—they will be your pride.

Does this mean that we should give up contemporary
literature, and live entirely in the monuments of the past?
No indeed, for nothing helps thought like *hic et nunc* questions, and if you do not belong to your own time what time
can you belong to? We should read modern poets and
modern novelists and follow art in its most advanced
manifestations. There must have been towards 1840 suspicious old Londoners who refused to read the *Pickwick
Papers* because the book was so unlike Mr. Addison's
Spectator. These old fogeys were losers. It would be as
foolish today to ignore Mr. Sinclair Lewis or Mr. Arnold
Bennett, even if we suspect that, in eighty years, they will
not appear like the Dickenses of the early twentieth century. On the other hand, if you try to keep up with the
industrialized literary production of today you will be
swamped and lost. Is there no way of making a selection?

There are dozens of ways, but here is an easy recipe.
Nobody can twit you with an affectation of indifference to
the present time if you leave out books which you find are
forgotten three months, that is to say, twelve short weeks,
after their publication. Do not read those. You will be
surprised to see how few there will be left to read. People
do not realize that the feverish excitement often produced
on the publication of many books, and which the innocent
public can hardly resist, is entirely commercial and arti-
ficially created by publishers. They imagine that the book
itself does it all. But the book does not do it, and the
publisher cannot do it longer than a week or two. When
ten more weeks have put their dead weight on the little
excitement it is more than forgotten. Draw up a list of the
American writers whose works published several years

ago are still on the shelves where the eye and hand occasionally travel. Those are the ones it would be unforgivable to desert, even for far superior reading, but you will see how few they are. Notoriety, high as it is above mere publicity, is still many degrees below fame. If a man reproaches you for ignoring books that have not made their author famous he is speaking from publishers' blurbs and ought to be listened to accordingly.

All that has been said above applies to literature, and literature, especially the higher kind of poetry which ought to be the staple of every cultivated reader, certainly provides a man with the most accessible thought he needs. However, literature is not our only field. Philosophy, the sciences, contemporary history and what are called the moral sciences, all put in our way explanations of the world and of man which are eminently thought-productive. In fact, they lead by a straight way to generalizations which are thought reduced to its most portable form. Now, it is true that philosophy, history, and the sciences have, as well as literature, their classics which cannot be ignored. Plato or Darwin cannot be absent from our library. Yet, it is especially in that domain that it is not only permissible but imperative to look for the most up-to-date information, acquired through the most modern methods. The history of the past interests us only in so far as it illuminates the history of the present. The politics and economics of today, the characters and ideas of contemporary leaders, the tendencies of modern parties are what we must endlessly revert to. We must be able to take out a map of the world and read frontiers and their problems like a book.

The same can be said of philosophy. The position *today* of the eternal problems means more to us than their solutions even in the great past. Religious questions ought to be studied in their latest exponents. So, of course, should plans for social reforms. So, above all, should the philosophy of the sciences.

Great books, great men, great problems and great doctrines, great facts and their lessons, all that is opposed to *'tits détails* cannot but result in high thought. The busier we are, the more severe our selection should be. Many men absorbed in business show such a rare quality of culture that we are surprised at it. The reason invariably is partly because hard work and even the weariness it leaves carry a nobility with them, but also because there is no room in such lives for inferior mental occupation.

Parents anxious to give their children the best of everything should as resolutely pack away trash of all kinds from their reach as if it were poison. It is surprising that intelligent people anxious to do their best should not realize that no book ought to be left in the nursery that is inferior to *Robinson Crusoe, The Arabian Nights,* or Perrault's *Fairy Tales.* You do not wish your children to be too clever? You do not want them to be like the twelve year old mature little women of the eighteenth century? Open the window, listen for one instant to the young people's conversation out on the lawn this week-end, and you will be reassured. Only too glad will you be if you can teach them to prefer distinction to vulgarity when they see it. Joseph de Maistre tells us that his mother used to recite Racine's verses to him when he was a little child and "his ears, having thus early drunk in such a nectar, ever after rejected sour stuff." A rare result!

d) HOW TO READ IN ORDER TO THINK

The title of this chapter would have sounded incomprehensible to an Ancient or even to a man of the classical ages. To them reading meant thinking. So, once more I

must insist that the notion—and the habit—of reading as
we absent-mindedly listen to the soporiferous brook belong
to a period of mental decadence. The consequence is that
they must be eliminated from the background of anybody anxious to think. I have been tempted many times
to annex Schopenhauer's maxim in his *Paralipomena*:
"Do not read, think!" or to transform it into: NEVER
READ, ALWAYS STUDY. A harsh saying? Not if we
realize that we should study nothing that does not interest us, and that studying only applies to the most enjoyable way of extracting from that what will interest
us the most. In precisely the same way does an artist study
a beautiful face instead of merely glancing at it. We can
never repeat often enough that nothing intellectual can
be achieved against the will of Minerva, that is to say,
in a field that does not attract us. Working in our vein,
without a sense of effort, and, on the contrary, with a
sense of ease and freedom, is the fundamental condition
of a healthy mental operation. Do not tackle algebra
when you are attracted by comedies, and if farces attract
you more than comedies leave comedies alone and study
farces. Only STUDY them. You will not have done so
long before discovering that there is more and deeper
pleasure in studying *le Misanthrope* than in rehearsing
Scapin.

This being laid down as a principle, how should you
read? As you please. If you please yourself by reading fast,
read fast; if you read slowly and do not feel like reading
faster, read slowly. Pascal does say that we are apt to read
too fast or too slowly, but he only blames an excess. (Lev-
ity is foolish to read too fast, but seriousness will be a
gainer in many cases if it reads briskly.) Montaigne com-
plains of a formal way of reading. "My thoughts go to
sleep when they are seated," he says, "so they and I
walk." Honest industry merely jogs along, curiosity flies

on Mercury's pinions. Passionate reading not only flies, it skips, but it only does so because it can choose, which is a high intellectual achievement. How do you read the time-table? You skip till you come to your place, then you are indifferent to the whole world and engrossed by your train, its departure, arrival, and connections. The same thing with a map which a motorist lends the anxious cyclist at the cross-roads. The latter's whole soul is in his reading. The same thing with a financial tip in a letter which a friend is waiting for you to return. The same thing with any formula for the production of the philosopher's stone. Whatever we read from intense curiosity gives us the model of how we should always read. Plodding along page after page with an equal attention to each word results in attention to mere words. Attention to words never produces thought, but very promptly results in distractions, so that an honourable effort is brought to nought by its own ill-advised conscientiousness.

A friend of mine, a celebrated French writer dealing in very serious subjects, has always seemed to me the typical active reader. He writes his books for himself and prepares them for his own pleasure. If he scents the least danger of boredom he studies the suspicious objects at long range, as a sea-captain observes an iceberg, and reports about it hurriedly and disgustedly. If, on the contrary, a subject, or an aspect of a subject, charms him, he approaches it tenderly and carries on a sort of exquisite dialogue with it. Not with you. You and I do not count much. We are admitted to the library in which the author bustles from his table to the shelves or back, we overhear the humorous, admiring, or impatient remarks he utters as one volume after another is pressed into the service of the then favorite idea, but all that we get, apart from this reflected pleasure, is an occasional wink when our unnecessary presence chances to be remembered. A delightful writer, yes, but a perfect reader. He never reads slowly; he never reads dully, he never reads sleepily. Like Montaigne, on his legs all the time, ready to fly from the book, as we do from a bore, the moment the book ceases to be fascinating. There is a gulf between that way of reading and what we have been given to understand is the serious method, viz. what du Bellay called "Keeping the chair warm," but Henri Brémond is right.

Does this apply to all kinds of books? Should a poet be read as *Who's Who?* Sometimes. Tischendorf once read the New Testament like that while two Roman prelates tried to keep him from the Ms. with cheerful Italian chatter. But it is evident that it cannot be done often. Poetry, like a queen, sets the pace and we proceed as she dictates. So does the sententious style of wisdom in any language. Obviously we must make a distinction between what we read for our information and what we read for our formation, between what we want for our use and what we need for our development. History, whether it be the history of politics, literature, art, philosophy, religions or the sciences, facts and the conclusions from facts, whatever is best summed up in encyclopædias or easily reduced to textbooks, can never hope to be read better than as a snob reads *Who's Who* concerning a duchess or an actress. No attention to the book, no thought of the author, but the whole mind engrossed by the matter, and striving to annex it forever within a few moments. Information books, even Gibbon's or Macaulay's or Mommsen's histories, have a right to our respect, but they are tools and ought to be used as such. If we only need to read twenty pages let us not think ourselves conscientious —but rather merely passive—if we read thirty. If we only read to refresh our memory concerning a subject by merely glancing at a chapter we have mastered before, do not let us waste time by rereading every word of it, or, if possible, let us substitute our notes for it. Boys are told to mind their book. They ought also to be told to think and not read, or to read with one eye shut and the other only half opened, so that they will read in their memory while the book will act as a mere prompter. Why read a whole page if two lines give you a sufficient idea of it?

Many books can even be read from their Table of Contents. The title gives you of course a general idea of their subject. Ask yourself how *you* would treat it, what your main line of argument would be. Refer to the Table of Contents. If it is not one of those farcical affairs which say "Chapter X: Emerson, Chapter XI: Nietzsche," and of which publishers as well as authors ought to be deeply ashamed, a quick and interesting perusal of the seven or eight pages will tell you at once what you can expect from the new-comer, where you ought to look for the information he has to give, and where you are sure to dissent from him. Reading in that way does not put you to sleep, it does not leave on your mind shadows of ideas that you would be glad to be rid of, it keeps you wide-awake as if the book were a living author which, as much as possible, it ought to be.

Books are not well made. If their authors were anxious to be useful, they would develop some imagination in trying to serve the reader instead of strutting to him. They often realize quite clearly that the statistics or the diagram which they are themselves using would appeal much more directly to the reader than page after page expanded from them. But they are not independent enough or serviceable enough to give them to us in their nudeness. Péguy was regarded as eccentric because he used typographical artifices to make his meaning clearer, and until recently a semi-colon at the end of a paragraph was considered a heresy, even if it was full of significance. Too copious a table of contents is discouraged by publishers as injurious to the book and over-helpful to the reader. The whole concept of a book ought to be modified.

In many cases you will get more out of a secretary's or a friend's analysis of a book than out of direct reading. For you will be questioning, which is the virile intellectual action, and the other man will be alert. Busy people who have recourse to this quick way often surprise us by the amount of their knowledge. King Edward VII, who never read anything, was, however, up-to-date in two or three literatures: shaving, dressing, smoking, he would ask questions of intelligent people or have significant bits read out to him, a truly royal highway to knowledge. La Bruyère alludes to it when he says: "The children of Kings know everything without having learned anything." Oral teaching is the most human and the most profitable of all. The effort made in America to create "community learning," or the growing habit of putting students in informal contact with thinkers is in the right direction. People are sometimes surprised at the results obtained by what they call "mere crammers." Those results are due to the superiority of methods making the student's mind more active than it has ever been. Two students "quizzing" each other the week before an examination may, for the first time in their lives, know what mental alertness means. If crammers' methods were used in the regular schools where sleepiness is often canonized as broad general culture there would be no need of cramming establishments.

At twenty, a man taught according to these methods ought to know the essentials of even the encyclopædic knowledge of today. He ought to have given himself or bought himself from some specialist as good a memory as he can ever get. He ought also to have acquired the habit of making notes without which Sainte-Beuve says people read as they eat cherries. If this way of approaching books should become popular, as in time it must inevitably be, mankind would cease to consist of an immense majority of minors.

This decisive, rather aggressive way of asking a volume: "What have you to declare?" leads in a brisk way to information. But formation or culture cannot be reached by the same high-handed methods. They require more time, more love, and an admixture of criticism and humility which is more easily discovered through experience than defined in words.

Writers dealing with the soul in its subtler and more recondite operations, poets, dramatists, moralists, psychologists (even using such fiction as *Adolphe*), religious or spiritual authors all create round themselves a zone of respect of which we are soon aware. The tone and gait of their very first sentence warn us at once that here the *sturm und drang* method cannot be used. Comprehension must take the place of mere intelligence, which means sympathy, reverence, and no haste. A medievalist may know all that can be known about the Cistercians, Vézelay, and plain-song, and yet raise his eyebrows on hearing a less erudite person say that some celestial antiphons to the Blessed Virgin or the mysterious light under an arch joining two uneven vaults make him realize the spiritual life of twelfth century monks. It takes multiform experiences of musical or architectural enjoyment, added to a sense of spiritual beauty, to understand a statement of such quality.

On the other hand the words in which it is expressed may enter an intellect and stay there, fashioning and dilating it till they are understood. A rhythm, an image, a thought, thus contained in a few words, may be enough for a meditation which the incidents of life may suspend but not interrupt. I have never forgotten, and certainly I have never exhausted, one verse of a ballad I once heard a few poor children singing over and over outside my window.

Un jour l'amour nous blesse.

These children's voices were careless and mocking like life itself, yet there was a touch of compassion in their insistence on the longs in the iambs which once in the ear would not go out of the soul. Of course there is an abyss between the human language conveying mere information and poetry of this kind. In order to be fully understood poetry has to be re-thought and felt over again, and this cannot be done by any mind without something personal being added to what we are pondering. When technicians speak of "Creative Criticism" they mean this reconstruction of a great thought. Creative criticism ranks with the highest kind of literature and with the higher kind of thought which we are to study in Part IV.

e) COMPREHENDING AND CRITICAL READING

Whatever we read we must first comprehend and, when we have comprehended, criticize.

Comprehension is the first and essential step in reading, but a vast majority of readers do not care to take it. They understand or think they understand what is obvious: the rest they regard as a mistake or a freak of the writer. I once tried a number of readers with that passage in *Aurora Leigh* in which Mrs. Browning defines philosophy as "sympathy with God" (II, 293). Only one of them seemed to think there was anything arresting in this phrase. The others visibly were carried away by the rhythm or dazzled by the superficial abstraction of the passage. When invited to fix their attention on this "sympathy with God," most of them first said it was farfetched but perfectly intelligible. But, being asked what these perfectly intelligible words meant, they had to admit they could not tell, and only two or three wished to hear. None ventured on any conjecture or tried to hit upon one. Their attitude was the uneducated one implying that if people use any except everyday language, they ought not to hope to be understood.

There is an abyss between people who want a poem to be as accessible as the morning paper and people in possession, or in search of, culture. Scholars often spend years over a retrieved fragment of a lost writer and read into it or infer from it the most interesting information. I have seen Angellier refuse after an hour's effort to give up an obscure passage of Herbert and succeed in making it appear laden with meaning yet clear to minds used to the rich language of poetry or philosophy. Certainly the habit of French lycée professors to devote a whole two hours to twenty lines of Seneca is first-rate intellectual training. Foreign visitors who, at first, wonder at this method ultimately appreciate it, and boys or girls compelled to use it are never slow in recognizing its merits. If you happen to know two languages, try your hand at really intelligent and artistic translation, were it only of four lines every day. The habit of complete comprehension will be a magnificent reward.

Too slow, you say, and too hard. But are we not endeavoring to think?

Criticizing is only another aspect of the effort to comprehend. The word in its etymology means "to judge," and in fact we think of a critic as a competent, not a carping, judge. The capacity to resist oral or printed affirmations, to have one's own opinion about an idea, a poem, a doctrine or a work of art, and to see it clearly enough to give it forcible expression is an exception. Most people suspend their judgment till somebody else has expressed his own and then they repeat it. Common parlance alludes to this weakness in the frequently heard phrase: PEOPLE DO NOT THINK. These four words describe the mental cowardice or sluggishness which makes sheep of most people. Such passivity cannot be too early counteracted. If it is done methodically and intelligently it will never produce overconfidence, only the youthful mind will acquire strength during the all-important formative period.

Teachers should attach the greatest value to the school exercise called literary analysis. The student is placed face to face with a literary piece worth while and examines its construction. This means reading and reading it over again, grasping the main idea which gave it birth, and observing how this idea is sustained throughout its development. The first time a boy or girl does this without any school preoccupation and realizes that a moderate amount of attention is enough to accomplish it he becomes an adult at once. Many remember the wonderful sensation of unexpected growth ever after. History, the estimation of a great period or of a famous man, the progress or regress of nations can give a teacher even a better chance than literature, more remote from the student's early experience of life. Testing a proverb or an opinion generally supposed to be right is equally useful.

The student must acquire the habit—which both Descartes and Schopenhauer regard as the fundamental philosophical attitude—not to receive anything as true or beautiful, but to consider everything *as a problem*. Mr. Chesterton also advises us to look at familiar objects till they seem strange, that is to say till we actually see them, instead of being suggested how to see them. Probably he remembers an experience which few people have not had. We are in the train or riding in a motor-car. The landscape, especially by moonlight, is unfamiliar and we note its characteristics with the interest of novelty. Suddenly some objects makes us realize that we have been mistaken, the section in our vision was perfectly familiar: we have only been deceived by the idea that we were elsewhere. At once, hills, trees and cottages shrink to a smaller size and we look at them with the contempt of habit. Our whole outlook on life and thought is vitiated in that way till we devote time enough and energy enough to a reëxamination of things as they are.

We should be given the habit of critical attention so that our first contact with anything worth the effort will give us as keen an impression as we are capable of. Do you not remember hearing the name of some foreign writer, Gorki, for instance, mentioned by friends long before you had an opportunity to read any of his writings? Your desire became keener in consequence. One day you chanced, in a magazine, on a fragment of the writer's diary, twenty pages on the return of Spring, with a beautiful narrative of a child's death, and an old bishop's visit. Each sentence, each word impressed, because of the intensity of your wish to make the most of these short twenty pages; there was, over the whole chapter, a mysterious charm like that of music or perhaps, perfumes. For a long time you refused to read anything else of Gorki's, fearing to break the spell and cherishing this chapter like a talisman. You realized that people who had read every volume of Gorki did not *possess* him as you did.

Criticism, when we read, think or feel in that way, is sure to be what it ought always to be, viz. the balance of what we should bow to with what we feel doubtful of. We do not insult great writers or great thinkers by submitting them to this test, but the reverse. Have you ever seen a painter, a real artist, watch in a gallery the masterpieces of his craft? What a difference between him and the effusive crowd elbowing him. His eyes, as he takes in detail after detail, have the hardness customary to a painter's glance; nothing escapes them. But suddenly the artist shuts his eyes and you know he is striving to project himself, so to speak, into the perfect picture. Do not be afraid to let a student accustomed to Shakespeare demur at calling Racine (who first wrote his plays in prose) a poet, if further examination makes him realize the perfection of the French dramatist as a painter of the passions.

Comprehension is criticism, and criticism or judgment is a mere synonym for thought.

f) HOW TO READ THE NEWSPAPER

Some people treat the newspaper with absurd respect, reading it through as if every syllable mattered. Others speak of it with contempt: "There never is anything in the newspaper: you waste time reading it." Others again —few in number—armed with a red pencil and big scissors sit beside a pile of newspapers which they treat unceremoniously indeed. Half the sheets are flung aside while the rest are eagerly but quickly gone over, the red pencil every now and then zig-zagging through a column. In less than an hour the seven or eight newspapers have been gone through and the red-marked pages alone strew the table, sofa and piano. Then the big scissors come into play. In a few minutes the clippings are heaped up apart, a neat little sheaf, while the litter of crumpled sheets is kicked aside till the maid can attend to it. Then the reader will be seen slowly going over his clippings, thinking. Nothing can look more different from the ordinary newspaper reader's expression than this pensive brow. A few moments afterwards the clippings will have disappeared, carefully tucked away in various dossiers.

You may see the same man again later in the day,

thoughtful and absorbed. His mind is running over the things he has read in the morning. You may meet him again in the evening. A circle of interested but silent listeners surround him. He is an unaffected, lucid and forcible speaker. Every now and then somebody asks him a question, one of those questions which causes everybody else to wish they could answer it. He does so, in a clear way, bringing in facts which you remember catching a glimpse of in the morning paper, but which you thought immaterial, whereas on his lips they actually give you the key to developments of vast importance: "This man thinks" you say to yourself.

What helps him to think? Simply taking the daily newspaper for what it really is: a page of history. Look for history in those ill-written sheets, you will think the thoughts of history; look for society, business or sporting news, you will talk the language of the tea-table, the stock-market or the field, but you will not think.

"I see. You advise us to treat the newspaper as a school-book."

"Precisely. Few schoolbooks can sum up as many events of world-wide importance as those which day after day have filled the newspapers since 1914. There never were such political dramas as those we can now follow. After Europe slowly regaining its balance, Asia is giving us a spectacular lesson. Meanwhile America, compelled by necessities of all sorts, is slowly being driven to the fore-front from which she has long been shrinking. Other ages have taken generations to produce the mutations we can see in a year. Indeed the newspaper is richer than any textbooks, and blind indeed must be the people who daily glance at it without realizing that if the quality of our thought depends upon that of the images we garner in, here is an incomparable chance. But blind are indeed most people, for the so-called wise and the foolish agree in speaking contemptuously of what they all read unintelligently."

The two foregoing sections have been an effort to describe:

1—The preparation of our lives and minds for higher kind of images.

2—The storing in of those images.

We now come to:

3—The elaboration of these acquisitions in the mind.

Chapter Nine

ELABORATION OF DATA IN THE MIND

a) GOING OVER OUR KNOWLEDGE

The son of the famous French painter Cazin, himself an artist of note, once told me that his father used to take him on professional rambles through the country. Every now and then the two men would stop for a few moments, sometimes only one minute; then, turning their backs on the landscape, they tested each other's recollection of the values registered during this brief interval. The older man's capacity for taking in and remembering was extraordinary. Sometimes he could, after months, prove that half-tints indistinguishable to the average vision were still clear in his memory. Cazin had learned this practice from Lecoq de Boisbaudran, who taught it to many other artists, Rodin among the number.

What artists do with color values we all can do with ordinary data. The test, or the thought of the test, makes our mental energy tenfold. Maroncelli, in his additions to Silvio Pellico's *Mie Prigioni,* relates how Pellico and himself, being deprived of books, pen and paper during the early months of their captivity, easily managed to give food to their minds. They would, sometimes singly, sometimes together, go over what they remembered, one day about history, another day about literature, another day again about philosophy. Supplementing each other it was surprising how much more they could remember than they had imagined. Gradually their knowledge, from being a useless chaos, became orderly and ready. Their minds simultaneously grew freer. They could, without pen and ink,

compose long poems some of which lived exclusively in
their creators' minds till at last freedom came. It is easy
to infer from Maroncelli's words that the two men thrown
back on primitive methods, no doubt also helped by that
exaltation of primitive sentiments which prisoners in the
Bolshevik gaols have similarly recorded, were nearer to
their souls and in fuller possession of their powers than
they had ever been.

We all can go through the same process, and no practice
can occupy empty hours or half-hours to better advantage.
The curious admixture of yearning and antipathy with
which most of us think of what we have learned at school
comes almost invariably from one cause. When we left
school we felt near knowledge, which was a joy, but since
then we have seldom found that we were any nearer
to it, and the consciousness of this creates a phantasm
with the usual impression of inferiority. Let any chance
offer to complete what never was entirely achieved and the
inferiority complex is promptly exorcised, and we experience exhilaration. Many a parent helping a child with
his *Caesar* has been delighted to find, and easily enjoy,
elegance where it had been merely glimpsed many years
before. Should *Caesar* have been read over again at college the result would have been the same, but *Caesar* was
not read at college: good-bye was said to it at school, and
it was left as an embryo of pleasure till an unexpected
chance occurred. The same can be said of practically all
that we have learned or skimmed through at school.

Go mentally over what you remember, completing it,
when necessary, by a few minutes' reading at home and
you will promptly know what education means. Was there
no book by which you were especially impressed at the
period of life when impressions were deepest because there
were so few? Is there not a poem you remember hearing or
learning and which, since that time, has remained in your

memory as the embodiment of poetry? Has there been
none since? I once saw a man take out of his pocketbook
a neatly folded clipping: it was a poem from one of the
magazines which this gentleman carried with him like a
talisman. There must be some poems that you too never
can forget. When you have a few minutes shut your eyes
and enjoy one of them as you may enjoy any dear memory.
Many a drab hour in the train, at an uninteresting hotel,
or on shipboard, has been brightened up by this habit as
a room is by a bouquet.

In the same way, we all remember moments, happy
crises which were the peaks in our mental life, introducing
strength where weakness used to prevail, or calmness where
there had been no rest. We can recapture the feeling of
those moments. When it enters our soul every fibre in us vi-
brates again as champagne sparkles to the touch of a
crumb. We imagined we were merely going over a chro-
nology of our own actions, and suddenly we find ourselves
in the productive portion of our personality.

We can also be profitably occupied with the recollection
of past travelling that is worth remembering. People nowadays travel too much and too early. One nail drives out
the other, and you hear philosophers of thirteen state the
fact with perfect indifference. Apparently less lucky people
are more fortunate. Charlotte Brontë, born within fifty
miles of the sea, saw it for the first time when she was
twenty-four, but the sight overwhelmed her, and a year
later she would allude to the experience as another might
allude to first love. There is something exquisite in remembering our first consciousness of being abroad, hearing a mysterious language, feeling far away, a little less
confident, and a little lost. The first thing that an Um-
brian town, a pine-surrounded cove in the Mediterra-
nean, or the Arizona desert, first seen in the solemn dawn,
told us ought never to be forgotten.

Artistic beauty should also be cherished. Why count the impacts of the track and calculate the speed of the train when we could have a perfect half hour remembering a room or two in the Louvre? With a little practice you can conjure up the *Venus de Milo* or the *Wedding of Saint Catherine* clearly enough to feel once more the fringe of impression which these works of art have left on you. Give yourself a little time, and the serenity of Greece or the luminous grace of Italy will be felt in turn. Without any effort you will not merely be going through a mental exercise but reaching the condition in which a Ruskin writes about art.

Great lives or great deeds can people any solitude. The lives of the Saints, above all, the life of Christ, have filled the existence of thousands of thinkers. French spiritual writers when describing this meditation use a remarkable phrase: *s'entretenir de la vie des Saints,* which means both carrying on a dialogue with one's self about those noble souls and keeping one's self alive by it. No word could be of a richer or more accurate psychology.

The ancients realized the virtue of this practice. Remember that Plutarch, who did more than anybody else, before the Christian writers, to make it popular, was a priest and a moralist, and his stories were the illustration of his doctrine. The passion for history which characterized the classical ages, and only decreased when artists took precedence over great doers of deeds, was fed by the admiration of exceptional individuals rather than by sheer interest in politics. In her charming memoirs Madame Campan says that Madame Louise, the youngest daughter of Louis XV, kept her busy during several months, reading out to her the history of France, because she wanted to have heard it through before joining the Carmelite nuns. When she adds "only one heroic action was possible for this princess and she did it," we realize that the examples of nobility gathered from that course of reading reacted on the resolution of this rare King's daughter. Anybody interested in the men and women without whom there would be no history, but only insipid uniformity, knows that, dead as they are, there is more life in them than in the automata we see walking around us. Thinking about them would be the natural impulse of most of us if the word highbrow or its synonyms were not terrifying a world of sheep into conformity. Every one of the mental exercises I have tried to describe has been not an effort but the most vitalizing relaxation to whoever has given them a chance.

b) REFLECTION

This is what people generally call thinking. When a person is neither speaking, writing, getting rid of some job, nor being spoken to, if he is also not asleep he is supposed to be thinking.

Reflecting is something more active. I said above that Madame de Maintenon defines reflection as "thinking attentively of the same thing several times over." This simplicity of language is delightful and expresses what it means to convey quite as fully as the scientific jargon made fashionable by the nineteenth century.

Certainly Madame de Maintenon's definition can be questioned, for it seems to imply mere repetition whereas various aspects of one proposition are sure to appear to reflection, but it is accurate inasmuch as it indicates the presence in the mind of one object engrossing it.

We all know reflection, at first spontaneous, gradually more deliberate and conscious. The moment a child is aware of fear or attraction he revolves in his little head the means of escaping from what is dreaded, or of securing what is wanted. This is done, as usual, by the presentment of images or sets of images showing to the mind pictures of what is likely to happen. Finally a sequence, a whole scenario, seems more probable than its rivals, and the intellect stops in its search after possibilities. This interruption is what we call a decision, as the picture finally retained sets our volitional powers in action. On the whole the object of reflection is invariably the discovery of something satisfying to the mind which was not there at the beginning of the search. There is no fundamental difference between this discovery and scientific invention. "How did you discover the law of gravitation?" somebody once asked Newton. "By thinking about it all the time," was the answer.

People are not often clear about this, because their best thinking is done when they do not suppose they are thinking, and consequently the successive phases of their thought can seldom be reclaimed from the subconscious. But every time we succeed in glimpsing the subconscious we do see the chain of images. Not infrequently we get up in the morning clear about an issue which appeared doubtful when we went to bed. If we can remember the last set of images overnight, comparing it with the one we are now satisfied with, we have no trouble in discovering the concatenation of intermediary images.

So, reflection is a natural condition, but only in the excitement produced by fear or desire. When this impulse is merely superficial it produces imaginative reactions also too superficial to be noted, which is our habitual mental state. If we have acquired a taste for reflection, or, as we say, meditation, or if some extraneous incentive makes us anxious to acquire it, we have to fight off our inertness in order to think. The morning meditation of pious people is a burden to them as long as it depends on a book for its support and has not become personal, that is to say, in plain English, egotistical. Otherwise we wait for the book, or for some director, to do the required thinking for us.

Children ought to be put through regular thinking exercises at school. The Montessori system arranges for intervals during which the children veil their little faces and think. Madame de Maintenon also recommended silent times, and the instruction I was referring to above deals with the methods for turning them to the best account. This experienced woman notes that the Saint-Cyr girls insisted on being given the solution of all their problems—even those set in play—and that "Please tell us" was more frequently on their lips than "Let me think."

Ask a class of thirty what is their explanation of any little subtlety interesting enough to fix their attention. Up will go most hands. Shake your head and insist on the query being answered in the copybook without any of the hubbub and excitement produced by it; in a few moments you will see on the more intelligent faces a smile meaning "I was going to talk like a fool and you knew it," whereas on the other faces you will see nothing at all. You will be lucky if one scholar in the group does any thinking at all.

I have seen classes positively tortured by a practice which however ought to be insisted on and the habit of which is soon acquired. Give the scholars a Latin text just difficult enough for them not to read it at sight— a pretty bit of Ovid, for instance—and lay down the following terms:

1) Not a single word shall be written down for forty-five minutes;

2) During the same period the dictionary shall not be consulted, but the text will be studied, and puzzling phrases will be scrutinized so as to make sense from the context;

3) At the end of the forty-five minutes the dictionary will be allowed for eight minutes;

4) Only then, shall the translation be written down.

I have never seen this method fail: it simply compels reflection. But boyish minds are so averse to it that the trial at first is an ordeal: the young fingers itch intolerably towards the pencil and the dictionary, because the habit is to get rid of the thing as quickly as possible.

The average scholar hates the composition of an essay because his past experiences have been anything but pleasant. He knows that after writing a few lines there will be a vacuum created by the necessity to write at all costs. If he were taught before his first experience that not a word of an essay should be written down till the whole of it is complete in the mind and *could be spoken in simple but clear language,* he would never know this degrading condition. Let him find by thinking out loud the subject in hand that nothing is so fascinating as to make up one's mind about something worth while, and that writing down the result of this investigation is of no particular importance but is sure to be easy, and the phantasm of an essay as a hopeless fight with vacuum will disappear forever. You can as easily dispel the phantasm of the superiority of books and of book-producers by pointing out that a volume is nothing but a sequence of individual chapters thus prepared, and that, as La Bruyère says, you can learn how to make a book as you learn how to make a clock.

c) WRITING AS A HELP TO THOUGHT.

The habit of using pen and ink in order to make up one's mind, just described and already mentioned in the chapter dealing with concentration, should be preserved through life. It is useful not only as a help to reflection but as an important element in an all-important inventory.

There are many questions which we regard as vital, yet about which we are vague. God, immortality, the foundation of morals, the nature and basis of happiness, love, marriage, the use of life, education, literary or artistic principles, what do we know about all these? So little that it is next to nothing. We have heard these issues mentioned so often, we have mentioned them ourselves in so many occurrences that we gradually acquire an idea that they are familiar. But this is a mere fallacy, the same under which we labor when, after long putting off our examination of a practical issue—which however happens to be puzzling enough and serious enough to haunt us—we finally come to a decision. We then imagine that we have somehow been weighing the *pros* and *cons* more than we realized, and we call our procrastination the time we have taken to think. But as a matter of fact we have not been thinking at all, we have only been wishing to think. If we could add up the minutes we have devoted to a critical examination of what we hold, say about a future life, we should be shocked at the ridiculous sum. Thousands of allusions from ourselves or from others to immortality do not make up a thought, they only mean that immortality is an important problem which people cannot let alone. I know a high ecclesiastical dignitary who has always wished but always postponed studying his cathedral which is one of the famous ones in Europe. Whenever I hear him say "my cathedral" I always think: "No, you do not own that cathedral, the cathedral owns you." So with those great questions of which we truly say that we are possessed without daring to hint that we possess them.

There are in the daily press a number of writers, male and female, who make it a point to have an opinion about everything. Day after day, four or five hundred words from their pens appear in which they express their views on an immense variety of subjects, most of them interesting. An expert runs little risk of erring in estimating how much time these fellow-writers of his have devoted to each individual question. It can be counted in minutes rather than in hours. The authors have seldom referred to any literature, even to an encyclopædia, they have been satisfied with summing up their own flimsy knowledge of the data and their flimsier impression of them. Yet, this is so much better than nothing that we read the articles through.

It would be a great beginning if we too would do that, limiting ourselves to recording what we know, what we are doubtful about, and what we should like to know. It might be enough to place us on the high road to knowledge, or, at any rate, understanding. Seventeenth century people used to enter such meditations in a copybook to which, from time to time, they would add fresh information. Today we take some wrapper and put in it the note which, like the parent crystal in a solution, may give solidity and order to our thoughts on the subject. The results are surprising.

Seventeenth century people also used their pens with similar effect to make up their minds about living men and women. These portraits were likely to be too elaborate, but they made observation and criticalness a necessity, and some of them, written by almost unknown people, have been valuable to the historian. Try the method in the interest of your nearest friends, or in self-defence, or from mere curiosity, and you will soon be conscious of an insight into your neighbors' souls which years of passivity had never given you.

Does it follow that professional writers stand the best chance of thinking their best? Not necessarily. I said, in Part II, that the professional writer is in danger of being a prey to many phantasms. Controlled sensitiveness belongs only to the very greatest. Average talent is constantly hampered by over-sensitiveness. The notion that one is writing for the public, for criticalness and often for misinterpretation, produces ill effects from which the person writing only to help his powers of concentration is free. But this inevitable drawback is conpensated by the vitalizing influence of composition. Even a mere journalist, if he is worth his ink, will often begin an article solely because he has to write it, but, in a few minutes, will enjoy the work because it sets his faculties free and gives them unexpected play. The mind is an enchanted spot where you are sure to be visited by fascinating apparitions as the nightly fisher on a marsh is sure to see will o' the wisps.

This is not all. There is no good or even passable writing, without some sort of outline destined to guide the pen. While producing these sketches, entirely similar to the preparatory work of an artist, the writer thinks no longer for his readers but for himself and is sure to produce of his best.

There is a time in life when the writer is independent of his reader, whose approval he does not doubt, as well as of his predecessors whom he regards only as precursors, and when he can sweep aside the most dangerous phantasms with a mere thrust of his pen. Fortunate are the writers who, like Byron, Shelley, Barrès, and a number of the philosophers, began to publish their thoughts when still in their teens or barely out of their teens. Those are not tormented by the phantasm that "all has been said." All the great commonplaces which go on intriguing the world, as they intrigue children, seem to them novelties which nobody has as yet looked in the face as they do. *Pereant qui ante nos nostra dixerunt!* Whatever they think seems to them worthy of expression and even of publication. And they are largely right, since no two musicians can ever play the same piece identically. As they proceed in life their youthful thoughts solidified in print surround them like a bodyguard and protect them against doubts or diffidence. A man like Barrès who was only separated from timidity by exceeding confidence might have consumed his powers in irony if he had not begun at nineteen to regard all his thoughts as poetry.

d) PRESERVING ONE'S THOUGHTS

To keep no track of what one learns or thinks is as foolish as to till and seed one's land with great pains, and when the harvest is ripe turn one's back upon it and think of it no more.

Some people have extraordinarily retentive memories and can do with a minimum of notes, but phenomenal exceptions do not count. Most men who have made a name in literature, politics or business have found it necessary to have a paper memory and those who have thought it possible to dispense with the drudgery of forming such a one have inevitably some day rued it. For humorists who define memory as the faculty enabling us to forget only emphasize an unfortunate truth. Striking or vivid impressions which we imagine can never be effaced from our consciousness do not survive in it more than a few weeks, sometimes a few days, unless something is done to give them permanence. A busy life teaches even congenital idleness to do that. Anybody whom his fate compels to use his brain actively soon realizes that he cannot afford to lose any of his resources, and he devises some plan for stopping waste. If he is rich enough he buys the assistance of a trained secretary. If not, he reads the books in which the methods of erudition or those of business (they are almost alike) are expounded, or he invents devices of his own. We marvel at the immense knowledge which some writers possess of what used to be called foreign politics but should be called at present the politics of us all. We wonder at the enormousness of the archives they must keep and at the difficulty for even them to find their way through that mass of papers. As a matter of fact, folio volumes of coarse paper on which clippings from the newspapers can be glued according to some happy combination of the vertical and the horizontal are all that is necessary. Red ink annotations will provide indication of richer dossiers. The secret is to clip all that seems important *at once*. Newspapers are historical documents prepared by men and women generally ignorant of, and indifferent to, history. An occurrence of far-reaching consequence may be mentioned in an inconspicuous column and in unemphatic type by so-called specialists who do not realize its importance and will never allude to it again. If the passage is not filed at once its absence may mean the loss of a capital link in the chain of events.

Facts are only the material for thought. Thoughts themselves, that is to say, the illumination produced in our mind by the presence of rich facts, should be preserved even more carefully. Certainly it is difficult and sometimes it may be dangerous—for it stops the working of the mind —to interrupt an intellectual reaction under pretence of noting it. But while the final result of mediation is before us we can rescue it from the fate of all dreams. The note must be brief enough to preclude the danger of what the Veda calls "putting words between the truth and ourselves," but it must be full enough to be clear to future, i. e., almost alien, re-reading. If we are conscious of an impulse to give a final form to an idea engrossing our mind it is foolish to resist or defer it. The best pages of a book are those written at a stretch under such an impulse. Many a writer compelled by life to do his work in spite of adverse circumstances has been grateful to himself for not giving in to laziness when the chance of thus fixing a glimpse or even a glimmer offered itself. He does not know the haunting and torturing phantasm that once his view of an object was higher and clearer than it is now.

Book-writing is the province of specialists, living is the business of us all. Moral life, sentimental life, religious life, whatever is above the *terre à terre* of mere existing, also consists of illuminations which once departed return no more. A diary, a few old letters, a few sheets containing thoughts or meditations, may keep up the connection between us today and our better selves of the past. I was deeply impressed as a youth by the advice of a spiritual writer to read one's own spiritual notes preferably to even famous works. All saints seem to have done so. The moment we realize that any thought, ours or borrowed, is pregnant enough not to be wasted, or original enough not to be likely to come back again, we must fix it on paper. Our manuscripts should mirror our reading, our meditations, our ideals, and our approach to it in our lives. Anybody who has early taken the habit to record himself in that way knows that the loss of his papers would also mean a loss to his thinking possibilities.

e) TYPE OF MIND PRODUCED BY THIS INTELLECTUAL DISCIPLINE.

I have known personally a great many men whose mental development has helped me materially in writing this book. Two of them have impressed me more than the rest for reasons which the reader will be told hereafter.

One of these men is a contributor to a famous magazine, a writer universally known for his knowledge of world politics and his *exposés* of them. His rich and luminous articles are eagerly expected by people interested in Eastern questions who have not had the same opportunities to go personally into them. They are discussed with respect by all specialists and, on more than one occasion, I have seen his views influence the attitudes of statesmen quite strongly.

The other man is a historian of religions. To tackle the history of religions with reverence and yet with independence, to secure a hearing on these questions from liberal critics without forfeiting the respect of conservatives, is a rare and difficult achievement. This theologian has accomplished it: the few scores of specialists who are interested in the same field show by their tone in discussing his views that they regard them as the outcome of a sincere wish to prefer the truth to opinion.

I have known these two distinguished men from the days of our youth, and to tell the startling but instructive truth, both of them used to strike me in those faraway days not as distinguished, but as rather the reverse. To use plain parlance, they were ordinary. To be sure, they exhibited the qualities of the plodder—what obituary notices call indomitable energy—and nobody ever dreamed of denying them more than their share of common sense. Also they had that peculiar sort of ambition not easily discernible from a taste for distinction which ultimately must raise a man above his original triviality. But their innate characteristics were ordinary. When I meet them, even now, my first impression is still an uncomfortable feeling that they may ruin the fabric of my respect for them by saying something irreconcilable with the high opinion we all entertain of what they write. They never do, yet I am never quite satisfied that they will never do it. Sometimes, I notice a smile, sometimes a tone of voice, sometimes a turn of phrasing which makes me feel on the brink of the abyss. But nothing happens, and I never knew anybody not familiar with these men from boyhood who was the least inclined to feel as I do. Nobody speaks of them as geniuses, but practically everybody regards them as a credit to serious literature. I know that their original angle was narrow, yet they show a constant interest in the higher issues, and when they do astonish a little it is by a too explicit aversion for trivialities. Their erudition is boundless. Visibly, they were born with excellent memories and stocked them with inumerable data ranging from philosophical views to mere human or picturesque details. I admit there never is anything unexpectedly piercing in what they say, but they know their own minds on a vast range of issues. They have come in contact with so many theories and have read so many discussions of them that arguments do not surprise or stagger them. Their arsenal is full of facts which the arguments have to take into consideration, or of counter-theories to qualify them. If all this were not couched in language from which all freshness is absent it would sound like the natural welling of powerful minds. For, there is a light radiating from all the hard facts they handle, and the illumination is enough to silence our inward reservations.

These men are the living demonstration that helps to thought, as expounded in the previous chapters, produce something so like thought as to be indiscernible from it, at all events enable a man to think his best instead of thinking his easiest. They were ambitious and hard-working, they substituted the pleasures of the intellect for what people call pleasure, they preferred the nobler issues to the less noble ones, and they chose to study methods. They are rewarded not only by the esteem of their peers, or by their subtle influence on events, but by the consciousness of possessing rare intellectual health and of using their powers with a minimum of waste. This result is well worth the initial effort of preferring something to nothing and of renouncing the universal vacuum.

More than once I have had opportunities to contrast these men with others, far their superiors in talent, whom I used to regard as predestined to brilliant careers. But the careers have been spoiled at the start and the rare faculties have dwindled to superficiality. Society, of course, is full of those failures which it seems naturally to prepare, but you will find them even in careers which apparently are their negation. Many promising young professors, physicians or lawyers have disappointed expectation and finally created disgust simply because they have accumulated obstacles instead of helps on the path of their thought.

What has been lacking? A taste for good books. These men have preferred light conversation, cards, or the idleness of the country club to what they were apparently born to love, and they have deteriorated in consequence. Saint-Simon shows us a gallery of such failures described with ruthless brilliance, but we need only look around us to see the living replicas of them.

You will say: knowledge, information are not the same thing as thought, and the art of educating one's self cannot be the Art of Thinking. Certainly not in the case of genius. But providing one's mind with the best food and with the best hygiene surely is the only way for average faculties not to nullify themselves. Take away data, and darkness will replace brilliant spots. Do we not say that God KNOWS everything, instead of saying that He understands everything? Imagine the difference in intellects like Malebranche's or Rousseau's if they had been less satisfied with their own phosphorescence and more eager for legitimate working. And who can doubt that the difference between such an age as the seventeenth century, all serenity, and our own, all nervousness, arises chiefly from the equipment of the former period? What gives cynical Frenchmen that strange political naïveness, at which foreigners marvel, if not a lack of information? What made Bossuet, a genius, inferior in controversy to Richard Simon, a mere scholar, if not disparity in knowledge of biblical questions? No amount of genius will replace facts where facts, and not genius, are necessary. On the other hand, complete mastery on the data of a question will give a man beside thoroughness that rapidity of argument which we cannot help calling brilliant thinking though, in reality, it is only information.

f) FURTHER APPROXIMATION TO ORIGINAL THOUGHT.

I have purposely chosen, to illustrate the value of the methods suggested in this Part III, two average specimens raised above their apparent possibilities by self-imposed training. But the same training applied to real talents produces results which fill the historians of literature. No better type can be chosen to represent these than Ernest Renan.

Renan, we all realize, was not a genius. Neither as a philosopher, a scholar, or a writer can he be compared with truly superior men. Yet, what intelligence! What insight and what outsight! What an introduction such a book as *Marc-Aurèle* is to an intelligent reading of history! The transformation of the meaning of the world "intelligent" and the halo that has simultaneously attached to it date from Renan. When M. Lanson writes of Victor Hugo that it is pitiful to realize that such a genius was not intelligent we know at once where the critic found the nuance he is so daringly emphasizing. Renan, more than men of greater power, remains the type of the capacity for comprehending. A host of disciples—among whom Anatole France and Jules Lemaître are the best known,—have shown how easily the method can be learnt and how certain its results must be.

1. Whoever has read the best books—not exclusively the classics, but the critics and scientists of the past two generations—has acquired not only information but a method of thinking. Intelligence is as contagious as gracefulness and wit used to be in the eighteenth century. This is not all. Taine used to say that thought is a collective, not an individual process. When we speak of "the mind in the making" we mean the same thing: doctrines are tested and developed, methods are improved, views are completed, the work of the whole world becomes the property of each individual seeker who cares to annex its results. In one word the volume of thought is growing.

2. Educated men who thus absorb the results of collective efforts are constantly made to see relations between ideas or between facts, and they take the habit of looking for such relations themselves. A modern man cannot think of Mussolini without thinking also of Napoleon; France after 1871 helps him to understand certain aspects of the German mentality after 1919; the colonizing methods of Britain throw light on those of Rome and conversely. Renan does this on every page. His nimble mind is everlastingly traveling over lists of data which he juxtaposes or, on the contrary, opposes and this active treatment of them produces light at every step. Signor Ferrero's habit of visualizing the present in the past and constantly suggesting the process by his choice of words shows the same method. It is indeed the method of all modern historians, and it cannot be denied that the results are immeasurably superior to the purely narrative method of former writers.

3. This habit of never seeing a thing without visualizing another beside it, or behind it, has in it something vital which makes it akin to the methods of the dramatist. Re-

ceptivity and imagination are constantly called into play. Many cultivated men and women spend delightful hours resurrecting the past, reconstructing a great historical fact, hearing a great historical character talk, testing a philosophy by its probable practical results, or imagining the future. All the time creative imagination is at work.

What is that, if it is not THOUGHT, and yet, it is within the possibility of innumerable people. Let them keep away from trivialities, and, instead, stock their minds with knowledge worth while; let them range freely through this mass of data, and thought will be actively produced.

"What a shame; there is such a lot in these chapters that I like: solitude, Spinoza, music, exhilaration and elevation, methods for not forgetting any more, a sort of easy way of making life, why, yes, of making life useful as well as beautiful. Yet, I am disappointed. Shall I tell you the truth? I honestly thought that this Part III would give me a real recipe for thinking. I mean some quick way of making my intellect active and fascinating, a Coué method of doing it all at a moment's notice. . . ."

"Or tabloids. Yes, it is a shame that thought-lozenges do not exist. I should buy some too. Well, can't you take strong tea, and lie down, as section a of chapter I says and see if your problems will not simplify themselves? Or, can't you sail for Italy and never open your mouth till you sight Naples? Nothing can be easier and it does the trick, the book says."

"Oh, yes, but it does not. What does it are good books, and reading only masterpieces, and never reading, always studying, in short, a regular mental Battle Creek treatment which I know I can no more submit to than to the real one. Yet, I know that if I should go over these chapters again, I should hit upon dozens of things which, as I read on, I have been longing to do. I love the Julius Caesar

little girl, and I abhor 'tits détails, *always did, I think, for if I were really frivolous I should not be reading this tantalizing stuff. Only, how I wish things could be as easy as they sometimes seem!"*

"You hate *'tits détails,* that is to say, commonness and obviousness, and you love solitude, Spinoza, Carthusian monks in white cells, good books which nobody else will read, Roman history and rare little girls, music and philosophy and sober enthusiasm. All this means that you are a perfect reader for this kind of book, an exceptional candidate for real thinking. What you object to is mental hygiene, adding up intellectual calories, and so forth, is it not?"

"Exactly. You describe it all as if you felt as I do. Yes, hygiene is hateful. Give me ten surgeons instead of one dietist. I am ready to strike the bargain, chloroform and all."

"No, you do not hate hygiene. I see you riding that grey mare every Tuesday. What you are afraid of is only the accumulation, the avalanche of restricting advice. In fact, what you seem to enjoy in this book is advice. You treasure each counsel as it comes, but when you try to remember the hundreds of them, down they come upon you like a landslide. Well, suppose you take one at a time, and for a while forget the rest. Suppose you begin with reading the *Times* as a page of history and . . ."

"Oh yes, I'll do that. I am sure I can do that. Don't tell me any more, and do not tell anybody else. I want to see how it will work with me."

"Work! You certainly do not doubt that wisdom works. So give the *Times* a chance, and please, henceforth, only read one chapter of this book at a time. The tabloid idea lies there."

Part Four

CREATIVE THOUGHT

Does "creative thought" mean genius? Yes, but remember that any creation, of any description, by the humblest artisan as well as by a superman, is the product of a state of mind which ought to be called genius.

Does it mean literary creation? Not any more than any other, and the reader ought not to infer from a paragraph or two in section 5 of this Part IV that the following pages are intended chiefly for writers. No mistake would lead more fatally to misunderstanding of the aim of this book. Its real object is to make thought, even in its highest forms and in any realm, accessible to all of us.

Chapter Ten

THIS IS A FASCINATING WORD. The notion of producing something out of nothing, or of substituting motion for immobility delights even children. There had been many half-draped statues of Venus before the *Venus de Milo,* but none producing such a powerful spiritual effect with just stone: we see it, and instantaneously we realize that a superior agency has been at work. Thousands of men have looked up wistfully at a vanishing lark; only Shelley wrote an immortal ode to it. Again, music worth the name means a wonderful creation. Our soul was vacant, and here it is filled with images and emotions produced by the most immaterial means. When we try to think of the Deity we soon discard infinity and eternity, as oppressive for our imagination, but creativeness we ponder on without any effort.

The reverence, frequently the awe we experience in the presence of genius, arises from the similarity between its gift and that attribute of the Godhead. We are constantly tempted to exaggerate our inferiority. We look at the busts of the great musicians or of the great philosophers; we notice the powerful brows, the searching eyes; we glance at our mirror and the consciousness of belonging to another race weighs us down. We read the lives or the letters of these exceptional men; we are not surprised to see them saying about themselves things which we should be ridiculous even to think about ourselves.

It is a good thing to read what has been written about genius and geniuses: their lives, full of splendid but thwarted efforts, act upon our minds as the lives of the saints act upon our spiritual faculties. We feel a sort of pride in them which testifies to our common origin and adds fresh vitality to our nobler desires. The presence of superior men is also a unique tonic. But it is futile to hope for an explanation of their gift; they are superior because they are superior, that is all. If you ask them how they are that, the answer will only be the laughter of Rabelais, and you will feel smaller than ever.

It is also dangerous to place these men on a pedestal and to adore a depressing phantasm in their shape. Literary men, poets, dramatists and artists of all sorts have been overestimated since one of them, Diderot, turned the whole capacity of a powerful mind to the exaltation of their gift. It has not been good for a man like Victor Hugo, or, above all, for a man like Alexander Dumas, to be made the prophet of his generation. A phantasm, stronger even than they were, was created which compelled them to fall into attitudes.

Too often we forget that genius, too, depends upon the data within its reach, that even Archimedes could not have devised Edison's inventions. We also forget that genius is not genius all the time, although it is superior all the time. There were long intervals between Pasteur's major illuminations. Poets know inspiration, but they also know periods of aridity during which they live on hope, or faith, and memory. On the other hand, we humbler people, have our intuitions, our times for feeling on the crest of the wave, for thinking our best and doing our best. Let us foolishly imagine, while we are so favored, that our gift, after all, is not of the first quality, and the spell will be broken in an instant.

The partiality—to which I have just referred—of the eighteenth century for purely intellectual superiority has had baneful effects, especially in France. Voltaire and

Diderot had no respect for genius when incarnated in founders of religions and there are still too many people who prefer brilliance to goodness. Political or social reformers, diffusers of knowledge, great organizers in any domain; apostles and missionaries, captains of industry, the upbuilders of mighty fortunes, great generals or great sailors, are treated rather contemptuously by critics and pedants, though their mental gift is often as rare, and the intensity of their physiognomy is as striking as the gifts and the commanding foreheads of their rivals. Their creations are before us, and many of them will be mentioned in history. But is there a single community in the whole world in which there does not exist the tangible proof that a keen wish for securing a noble result, kept up through a lifetime of perseverance, must inevitably attain its goal? Why should such efforts be regarded as inferior to intellectual efforts, especially when, as is too often the case, egotism is glaringly visible in these? Who would dare to say that Florence Nightingale has not the same right to be regarded as a creator as George Eliot?

We may go further. All human lives of any distinction, even if no durable monument prolongs them, are creations, sometimes of an artistic, sometimes of a moral nature. There are kind, thoughtful men whose names will never be known to the world, but whose lives appear as masterpieces to those who knew them well. Those men were born with the faculties and the chances of us all, but they saw what could be made of them and accomplished it. The diary of a Joubert or the letters of a Cowper might never have been published, but the people who loved Joubert or Cowper for more than there is in their writings would be haunted to their dying day by the charm emanating from those retiring existences. Madame Récamier has been dead a hundred years, yet, more people stop in a reverie before her picture than before that of Madame de

Staël. She never wrote for the public, she never orated or prophesied, but the life she led in those three rooms at the Abbaye-aux-Bois is still an ideal for innumerable women who have heard of it. Can we say that this fascinating *aura* is not her own creation? And are not the saints as magnetic as geniuses?

Compare these people who did things, or *were* the thing, with those other people who never did anything and would have been nothing but for a modest capacity for writing up what others were doing. Which is the real creator, the person who creates inspiration or the one who only receives it?

Chapter Eleven

THE ROOT OF CREATION: IDEAS.

THE ROOT OF CREATION, whether speculative, artistic or practical is, of course, an idea. Gradually this idea grows, annexing or using its neighbors, and becomes a mastering purpose which cannot be resisted. Finally it results in some creation. Taine falls in love with a cat, gets fascinated by cats, treasures and cherishes innumerable memories of the seductiveness of cats. When he looks more the dried-up little old scholar than ever he produces the famous sonnets on cats. Another man has watched a stray cat in the streets: he has seen the poor little creature sometimes looking up imploringly at an uncomprehending passenger, sometimes pretending to itself that nothing is really happening and trotting along as if surely home must be round the corner. The vision acts through years. Another man might translate it into clumsy language, this one speaks of it in tender words which go to one's heart. In time a home for stray animals is the result.

Nothing can be simpler. Simplicity is the characteristic of all creative notions. The two Frenchmen who had the greatest influence on their countrymen during the latter part of the nineteenth century and the early part of the twentieth were undoubtedly Anatole France and Maurice Barrès. What acted on their minds before the philosophies they evolved reacted in their turn on millions of other minds? Anatole France looking at the starry sky was struck by the insignificance of man with his ambitions and passions, of the atom-Earth with its microscopic empires. Barrès, standing at his father's grave in Charmes churchyard, while the bell was tolling for Vespers and a solemnity was spreading over the village, realized the continuity between his ancestors and himself, as well as what he called the claims of the soil. Both visions filled the two men's lives, and are still the souls of forty volumes, and have influenced the thoughts of millions.

The problem obviously is how to have such soul-filling, life-fashioning ideas.

Our soul is an ocean. Its possibilities, its receptivity and elasticity are mysterious and seldom within our ken, but they cannot be doubted. What it stores up during our life is as mysterious, but it is as undoubtedly vast. Remember that the Alsatian old woman was eighty when, during her last illness, she began to talk Hebrew. It was sixty-five years since, as a little maid in the village Rabbi's home, she had overheard the master reading out *Genesis*. She was in the kitchen, she was not a Jewess, she did not care a straw, and yet the whole series of outlandish sounds had been preserved on one of the million records in her memory. Who has not been amused or puzzled by the reviviscence of an utterly indifferent sentence, heard years before, caused by a few syllables bearing a faint resemblance to it? The forgotten words fall on our ear, eerie but unmistakable. A strain of music, the odor of mignonette will unexpectedly revive in us states of mind from which, in childhood or adolescence, we shook ourselves free because their vague pregnancy made them as hard to sustain as their poignancy made them exquisite. Inspiration, the high-strung condition in which emotion, eloquence, music, or merely strong coffee can place us, reveals to us whole regions in our souls which have nothing in common with the sandy barrenness of our daily existence. Often too, in our lives, but more frequently at certain periods than at others, we are conscious that our intellectual vision is keener than people, or even than we ourselves, supposed.

We hear a conversation and, as the words cross one another, we register people's motives as if we were reading them. We go to a lecture and we appreciate or criticize it, as it goes on, as we seldom did before. We are conscious of all that flashes through our minds. Meanwhile we know that other, less perceptible, gleams may gather light if we watch them without pretending to do so, and a rare illumination may follow.

What we then see, what we sometimes note on bits of paper which we treasure like misers, are the germs from which creation springs, or from which a fuller life is developed. They may be short-lived and elusive, or jostled out of sight by a rush of others, but they do not differ in nature from what ultimately becomes, in highly gifted intellects, the work of genius. How they can be multiplied or strengthened, above all, how they can be got at when they have retreated to our subconsciousness, is the problem.

Chapter Twelve

PHILOSOPHERS WORTHY OF THE NAME all entertain the ambition of giving an explanation of the world. Most of them realize how much that is purely tentative there is in those attempts. On the contrary, most of them are emphatic in their recommendation of some mental process through which we can attain Truth. This word is getting worn out from over-use, and modern scepticism is on its guard against it. But nobody objects if it is understood to denote the illumination accompanying the contact of our mind with what we call realities. When we are conscious of such an illumination, our intellectual search is at an end and repose takes its place.

Intellectualists like Aristotle, the Schoolmen, Descartes, or most modern scientists look for this illumination in formal logic. They want a full and clear statement of data, and they set precise rules for their elaboration and the verification of the conclusions drawn from them. Their idea seems to be a scientific collection, well-housed in a roomy hall and arranged in such logical sequence that at no time is the visitor inclined to stop in uncertainty before the specimens displayed for his inspection.

There is another, quite contrary, method, which has always charmed people of a religious or poetic turn, viz. immediate contact with spiritual realities. A lyrical poet does not refer to encyclopædias when he feels the coming of inspiration. We, humdrum church-goers, are glad of a good sermon or a serviceable book to help us with our plodding meditation, but great mystics have no need of any such adjuvants: their minds are soon ravished, they do not know where, and they stay there, rapt in contemplation. That their minds are not the victims of a fascination, no matter how noble, but, on the contrary, follow the rules of some logic is made evident from the fact that, as appears from their writings, contemplation reveals substantially the same things to them all. The virtue of this mental process is also visible in their writings. The characteristic of mystic literature is sublimity, of course, but it is also a marvellous facility. Madame Guyon used to say she could write endlessly about spiritual realities, and she does not differ in this from safer guides than herself. No trace of effort can be detected in Saint Teresa's *The Castle of the Soul* or in the Fourth Book of the *Imitation*. Many passages in the Letters of Saint Paul are more lyrical than anything else. Compare the feverish tension perceptible in those of Pascal's *Pensées* which are merely the work of his intellect with the state of mind easily inferred from the few lines scribbled on his famous amulet, which was the outcome of a revelation. From Plotinus to Swedenborg all illuminists have descanted on the floods of light produced by the contemplative process in which they delighted. But is there a single man or woman who has not experienced something of the kind?

Modern Intuitionists, like Newman or Bergson, are closely related to Mystics. Men of such culture and such vast reading cannot but know the value of accurate information, but they believe in a superior logic making use of it. Pasteur was constantly visited by intuitions which he was afterwards at great pains to check by the ordinary canons of science. Such intuitions are not revelations, they are only the result of flashlike comparisons or oppositions of sets of images stored up in the mind and incredibly more elastic than the formulas in our intellect which Newman calls the "notional" as opposed to the "real." Read the *Grammar of Assent,* or *Creative Evolution,* and you will realize that here are the clear lineaments of an Art of Thinking, certainly depending more on experience and less on mere exposés than the advice given by Descartes, Locke, or Herbert Spencer, but aiming at exactly the same goal. A process of lovingly bending over one's consciousness is preferred to an exterior one, but the possession of rich pregnant notions is the end in view just as well. In the same way, it is difficult to read what poets say about their visitations, or what artists say about their art without realizing that these men, constantly bent upon turning their powers to the best account are in reality laying down for themselves the principles of an Art of Thinking. The writings of two typical modern men, Nietzsche and Barrès, constantly describe or exemplify a method for the production of thought.

Is it possible to sum up what all these introspectors say in an immense variety of ways? Yes. Read them, listen to them, analyze their methods, scan their attitude, you will find that they are living and thinking as close as possible to two fundamental precepts:

1. Be yourself.
2. Find yourself.

Chapter Thirteen

"BE YOURSELF"

"BE YOURSELF if you want to create anything original" is a truism. How can you do anything that will really be yours if you are not conscious of your own personality, if you are somebody else, or even everybody else, or if you are not quite the man you know you could be?

There are two main obstacles in the way of a man who wishes to be himself: pretence and diffidence. Few people are not hampered, or have not been hampered in some phase of their lives, by one or the other.

Pretence or pose is not confidence. Confidence, when it is associated with sterling qualities, is not mere confidence any more: we call it brilliance. Balzac poured himself out in conversation in a way which gave offence to people of an over-refined taste, but which delighted psychologists. The same fault is common in artists whose delight in their conceptions, and gradually in themselves, is irrepressible. All people endowed with powerful vitality or imagination, most people with a passion for independence which life has not damped too severely, are not afraid of forcing themselves to the forefront. Angle-Saxon simplicity, added to Anglo-Saxon belief in individual rights, produces similar results. People who think Anglo-Saxons taciturn or self-contained have seen them under some restraint, or have not lived familiarly with them.

Cynicism itself is not always a pose either. In its higher specimens it is only an exaggeration of sincerity tainted by conceit or by Rousseau's certainty that nobody is much better than one's self. I have always found pleasure in a witty Parisian Jewess's admission that "she would not be natural if she were not affected." Most people die without saying anything as terse. Marie Bashkirtseff, now that we have some portions of her diary in their entirety and not carefully edited by André Theuriet, may be a Queen of Flirts or a Queen of Snobs; she certainly is the author of one of the most sincere human documents we possess. Is there a more irritating book in English literature than *Evelina?* Yet, Frances d'Arblay's self-complacency is so marvellously transparent that after a century and a half the book has not been killed by its faults.

Pose is insincerity in a degree which makes it impossible that the pretender should not be aware of his own attitudinizing. It means playing at seeming to be what one is not. How could there be any vitality left for personal thought when it is used up in that comedy? How can a man hope to be a creator, even on the humblest scale, if he insists on being an actor? People who pretend they follow without difficulty an intricate debate, who pick up formulas thanks to which they can judge airily of literature and art, who affect to be experts in foreign politics because they have travelled and were in Geneva during the League's last session, who give themselves the airs of knowing people they have never met and say "my friend So and So" of a distinguished man they have met just once; the innumerable people who would think themselves disgraced if they were to say: "No, I have never read Walter Page's letters, but I read trash in bed every night"; people who applaud a foreign orator whose language they have never learnt—those people are actors, some of them as clever as any on the stage, but they will never say a word which somebody else will deem worth remembering, and they will never have a thought which will give them the hope of being better than mere gramophones.

Professional writers, by the score and the hundred, are

apt to be insincere and to lose thereby all their chances of honest improvement. Many of them are almost compelled to be so. They were sincere at first in their liking for literature but they had little to say, and when that little was said, they were not in a position to stop; writers they were, and to write they had. So, they do write, without any real impulse, on a multitude of subjects. They fill the newspapers, alas! Their jejune glibness, their dodging all that might commit them, their artificial humor do not take in, for one instant, even an unprofessional reader who wants information and is conscious he is not getting it, but, all the same, that way of writing is the great lullaby that puts the modern mind to sleep. Observe that even so-called specialists or savants can debase themselves by such tricks. I have read the works of medical or archæological experts who were expert above all at saying Yea and Nay in the same sentence.

Literary fashions are destructive of the writer's personality. How hot the French Romanticists used to make themselves by trying to climb up to Victor Hugo's heights! How much French wit must have perished in the darkness of Realism! How many writers between 1890 and 1920 copied the complacent rhythm of Anatole France without being able to rival his range of illustration, his sensibility, or even the quality of his naughtiness! Who can tell how much that is sterling observation of life or of the human heart can be destroyed by the mere affectation of a rhythm? Anybody who has tried his hand at a pastiche must know how strangely this amusement helps the special inspiration needed and what unexpected facility it develops in one, but is not this what happens with a farcical drawing-room imitation? The imitation of exterior qualities is detrimental to real creativeness, and, as Herbart says, ultimately becomes injurious to character. Acted, spoken, or written insincerity is *per se* destructive of personality and comes to negative results. The more we try to seem what we are not, the smaller our chance becomes of fully being what we really can grow to be.

Diffidence is the other fault that prevents us from being ourselves. It has a right to a great deal more attention and more sympathy than its counterpart.

Diffidence must be carefully distinguished from indolence which also frequently masquerades as modesty. Many people can never be themselves because they cannot stiffen long enough to be conscious of their own personality. They are the man they listen to, or the book they are reading: they are not themselves. In childhood, medicine or athletics can remedy this feebleness, for effort of any kind is enough to create a beginning of personality. Properly cultivated emulation or self-interest can also help education in its work of developing individual possibilities. Later in life, there would still be hope if the wish for individuality, or a vision of the bliss there is in the feasts of the intellect, could be conjured up. But they seldom can. Even catastrophes leave supineness unmoved.

Diffidence proper may be a form of conceit: better shrink into one's self than appear as one is, that is to say, inferior to what one would like to be. Often too, it is the consciousness that one is ill-prepared by natural inclination or gifts, by education, or by present circumstances to do what one is doing. Or it is the vague reproach of our conscience when our immediate preparation has not been what it might have been. A charlatan does not mind, but an honorable man, especially a man who lives more or less in the hope of some day producing beauty, is afraid of spoiling one more chance after many others.

Phantasms of all kinds naturally find an easy prey in sensitive natures. Artists are well-known to be what people who are not artists call ill-balanced. They may be pretty well satisfied with what they have achieved in the past: a poem, a chapter of a novel written by them several years before and beginning to be forgotten enough to seem like the work of somebody else, will often give them keen pleasure. But while this poem or chapter was being written it procured more annoyance than satisfaction. The artist constantly bears in his mind the idea of an impossible perfection. As he works, or just before he begins to work, his mind is full of elusive but the more fascinating images which he hopes to fix by words. The moment he endeavors to do so, or even tries to see these images more closely, they vanish, leaving only the fragments of expression with which he has begun to clothe them. Those remnants are enough to enrich masterpieces, but compared to the mysterious appearances which came before them they are like mere dross. Read Katherine Mansfield's *Diary;* you will realize what a writer whose every touch seems to be final went through, feeling that all she was doing, far from being final, was tentative and inadequate. The notions: "This could be expressed better" or "Somebody is sure to express this better" are paralyzing phantasms, and diffidence is a mild word to describe their effect.

Many times too, the artist will think of some rival he may or may not love, but admires, and imagine that this person would do the same work with wonderful ease and in far better style. Frequently he will be doubtful of his subject and regard it as inferior to several others which a little thought might soon reveal to him. He may have moral qualms too, imagining the practical effects of what he is producing on minds whose weakness or sensitiveness he exaggerates. Charlotte Brontë almost says that her conscience would not have allowed her to write *Wuthering Heights,* even if she had had her sister's inspiration for it. All these ideas, extraneous to the one which ought to monopolize attention, are phantasms obscuring the intellect and weakening the will power necessary for artistic achievement. Suppose enough of them, or a siege of one long enough to create a habit, and the man will not be himself any more, or will be himself in a diminished way.

What can be done? Dominique, in Fromentin's classical novel, just gives up, thinking it better to be himself as a gentleman-farmer than feel dwarfed as a poet. A desperate solution. Balzac, after his seventh or eighth failure, might have adopted it too and been satisfied with just being a printer, as indeed he was at the time. Yet, he was within a year or two of the inspiration which never left him afterwards. Perhaps the effort he made as a business man kept his will power up to the mark as an artist. Everbody will be benefited by going into some enterprise, charitable or other, in which responsibility of a definite character will be involved; by being in some fight for a real idea, and by speaking in public about it. The artist who is nothing else and feels phantasms sitting on his chest is a martyr, and ought to do anything to escape from the torture and humiliation.

Whatever method we resort to we shall find that any powerful ideal or idea in us cures diffidence and creates not only forcefulness but a magnetism. The moment we are conscious of any such forces filling our minds and our lives, we shall also be conscious of their irresistibility. So, the problem of how to be one's self is ultimately a moral problem: viz, how to make the best use of one's faculties.

Chapter Fourteen

"FIND YOURSELF"

To be one's self, in the last resort means, as we said, a stiffening of the attention or of the will. To find one's self means the reverse. We are not living with ourselves when we are too attentive to exterior things. We may feel the most conscious of our own personality when we are the most active, when we are straining every nerve in the pursuit of some object; but we never dream of saying that we are finding ourselves when we are in that busy condition. On the contrary, we are apt to wish for the end of it, and we long for a time of quiet meditation to possess our soul in peace. Languages are full of metaphors describing those opposite states of consciousness.

We "find ourselves" in any mental atmosphere recalling that of a course of reflections in solitude, of a reverie in the gloaming or in a quiet autumnal scene, or of a moral crisis which revitalizes without crushing us. We know times of intellectual intensity produced we seldom know how, but during which we feel segregated from the rest of the world, and yet in sympathy and understanding with everything. Some great book, the vicinity of genius or saintliness, music, are some of the causes, but there are many others, sometimes as unlikely as those producing hypnotic phenomena, which take us where our innermost is to be really found. The violinist, bending with touching fondness over his instrument, loves it, no doubt, for what it is giving him, but the soft radiance over his face means that beginning of ecstasy which is the ravishment of a soul into itself. All reflective, all productive natures tend towards such states.

When I was a very little boy my people used to picnic sometimes in a pretty Ardennes valley under a clump of oak trees shading the grey walls and discolored slate roof of an ancient mill. Before leaving, the party would visit the miller for a quarter of an hour, and the *salle* became a scene of unusual animation. I generally managed to slink out of it, unobserved, through an arch opening on to a stone staircase. There was next to no light on those steps at first, and what little there was made it look dismal and vaultlike. You went down and down the winding staircase at least thirty steps, the light growing stronger but of a strange green tint as you approached the bottom. Dripping sounds and the rush of swift water over pebbles were heard. Finally appeared the scene I had been longing for. A deep cut through the polished slaty strata, mosses and dainty ferns of all kinds hanging from every moist cranny; strass pendants over it all. On my right the broad wooden wheel seemed enormous and ferocious, and I would look away from it, knowing that I should be terrified if it should suddenly begin to turn and make its thumping noises while starting the stone and iron machinery upstairs. But running swiftly past, there was the brook, broad and shallow, marvellously clear and cool, catching every green reflection from the walls and a little of the blue up above. I would stay there for what seemed a long time, sometimes quite nervous, yet unable to leave. What I saw, what I heard, what I felt and thought in that magical place seemed to be more my own by right of discovery than anything else.

I have never been able to read about the stream of consciousness without remembering the miller's brook. We can only get at what is nearest to our most personal, viz., our subconsciousness, by leaving the hubbub of the world where it is and seeking in deep repose for what differentiates us from other men and women.

The following seem to be the most practical rules for succeeding in that search:

1. *Find your own vein.* Our vein means the stratum of our consciousness that is the richest, and which will yield the most. In other words, it means the objects, whatever they may be, about which we think our best. What are those? It is unfortunate to have to say that bad psychology, only too often influencing education, answers: they are the objects on which you expend the greatest amount of study. The answer, on the contrary, should be: they are the material for thought which you handle with the greatest ease and with the greatest enjoyment. It is impossible to reflect about the principles of an Art of Thinking without admitting to one's self that what one is endeavoring to do is to devise a method bringing us all nearer to genius. Now genius is primarily power resulting in ease. Genius never plods. When Buffon defines it as "a long patience" he means not the patience of doggedness, but the perseverance of enjoyment. Who will believe that, during the seventeen years of his quest after his law, Newton did not derive immense pleasure from what we wrongly call his work, but which ought to be called the fascinating occupation of his mind? Genius is well known to be able to devote longer stretches to its work than ordinary talent which needs intervals of relaxation. The reason is that the relaxation of genius lies in the consciousness of doing what it loves to do and would hate to forego. Pope, who once wrote:

of happy convents bosomed deep in vines,

might have parodied Shelley, but he never could have written the poem on the Euganean hills. Imagine Dickens writing society novels. Genius may be associated with other talents and its brilliance may deceive us by its multiform achievements, but we never mix it up with versatility.

What books do you read with most pleasure? On our shelves are some volumes which are our family, and others which are only visitors. Which are the first? What are those from which we catch ourselves mentally quoting to ourselves? What subjects keep us really interested? What are those on which we talk the most easily, and with the greatest pleasure, to ourselves and to others? Education, the unfortunate notion that an effort must be associated with everything great—a curious perverseness in many high intellects—are responsible for ridiculous delusions. Ingres preferred being complimented about his talent as a violinist to hearing about his genius as a painter. Falguière, the sculptor, would show visitors his paintings, but not his statues. One day Henner was being taken round the studio, and before every canvas would, to Falguière's delight, exclaim: Stunning! marvellous! Coming to a small marble which Falguière was passing by without a glance, the other artist stopped short and said with his Alsatian accent: "Ah! but this is good!"

What is nearest at hand is our vein, but it takes luck or experience to convince us of it. The Spanish crew who were becalmed in the ocean, off the mouth of the Amazon River, could not believe the natives signalling that the water all round their ship was good to drink and they had only to throw down the buckets. Far-fetched is a phrase which, in its broader sense, applies to most of what we do. Yet, we are all conscious that what we like best in a writer are the works reflecting the most naturally his own peculiar gift and temperament. Who reads Bossuet's uncouth poetry? We like things to give us the impression that they flow. Again, what writer does not realise that his most successful pages are the ones which gave him the least trouble?

2. *Speak or write in your vein.* As you sing on the breath. People in love or in anger, or possessed of some strong conviction or desire, are always eloquent. Few of us have not had some occasion to hear speeches, more stirring than those even of great orators, poured out by highly-wrought people who did not care a straw for eloquence.

Writers with a deep moral background of any description are well known to possess a richer vein than mere artists. Why do people nowadays prefer the violent ill-mannered Léon Bloy to Anatole France? What makes Léon Daudet, in spite of his prejudices, injustice and conceit, the Juvenal of this generation? Anybody drawing on a similar reserve will produce similar effects. People are right to make game of the exaggerations of Super-Realists. Mr. James P. O'Reilly, writing in *The Irish Statesman* about Mr. James Joyce, describes their method without any charity:

"Sit in a favorable spot where the mind can concentrate on itself—or on nothing at all. Get into as passive or as receptive a condition as possible. While thinking of nothing definite, write quickly whatever comes to mind —quickly, so as not to retain and so as not to rewrite. When you are conscious of influencing by reason what your hand is writing, begin again. Write, for example, a series of l's until the letter l unconsciously begins a word, and your thought series continues. There's the method."

Surely, this is the method of many practical jokers who call themselves Super-Realists, but it is not the method of some extremely talented young men among them, nor that of two of their most famous predecessors. Read Péguy's *Jeanne d'Arc,* an undoubted masterpiece which the author produced at twenty-two. Read most of Claudel's works, and you will know what is meant by writing in one's vein. All rising literary schools are the outcome of a mental experience showing a few born writers that freedom and naturalness are essential to inspiration. They all rediscover the same principles. I have said before that the Middle Ages owed their unique creativeness, in all the realms of art, to their freedom from phantasms. So did the French Romanticists till they became hampered by the phantasm of admiration. Super-Realists want to write from their subconsciousness, that is to say, as humanly, richly and freely as possible. Everybody wants to draw on that vein. When I hear that Racine, the perfection of his perfect age, used to write his plays in prose before transmuting them into the exquisite dramatic poems which foreigners find it so hard to call poetry, I always feel inclined to think that those first drafts were Super-Realist effusions, as different from *Phèdre* or *Athalie* as Flaubert's first version of *La Tentation de Saint Antoine* was different from the one he finally evolved and definitely spoiled. Have you never noticed the tendency of most artists to describe their first haunting view of their work in familiar, or worse than familiar language? A super-realist effort to keep away literary composition with its trammels and phantasms as long as possible.

Some rhythms—taking the word in its fullest meaning— keep the writer nearer his subconsciousness than others. The Homeric rhythm does it more infallibly than any other. You will feel it in Mr. Belloc's books, even if the author does not tell you, as he once admitted to me, that Homer is the only novelist he reads. You will feel it in Barrès' best book, *La Colline Inspirée,* about which I also had the author's own testimony. The habit of working on such a rhythm results in an almost physical sensation informing us that we are drawing on our innermost.

3. *Know the value of intuition.* An intuition is the mental act we produce the most naturally and with the least tangible alloy of extraneous elements. Suddenly an illumination flashes upon us which we had perhaps longed for, perhaps not. In one instant we see, as the word implies, what we had not seen before, and we become conscious of the repose accompanying certitude.

A solution of some difficulty which we have been fighting with, perhaps for a long time; the transformation, as by magic, of a whole situation which we had viewed in a pessimistic mood, now quite differently; a clue unexpectedly found to a person's disposition which used to puzzle us; the revelation of the something indefinable we call the physiognomy of a city; an idea for our work; a whole dramatic scene visualized as if it were acted before us; a strong conviction, like that which filled Pasteur and had filled three or four men before him, that a method which seems preposterous to others is however as sensible as it seems to us, are examples of intuitions. Hundreds could be found.

No strain, and on the contrary, a sensation of fulness and freedom are felt during those brief but dazzling revelations. If you have a gift for mimicry, you know that the moment you imagine yourself to be the other person, you require no effort to think, speak and gesticulate as he does. To an inferior actor this would mean prolonged study of each individual imitation, to one possessing this talent the whole thing is implied in the initial vision.

Intuitions are not always as rich as the ones just enumerated, they may only be rapid glimpses vanishing before we have had time to seize them and as tantalizing as they are fascinating. But fascinating they always are. They have nothing in common with the teasing apprehensions or the depressing doubts which often shoot across our consciousness in much the same manner. Some books, at times any book, will produce them. We then experience a curious duplication: we go on with the book because we love the illuminations accompanying our reading, yet we are on our guard against it, because we realize that if we should give it our full attention we should also interrupt the magic display it has caused but not produced. Hard pebbles would be substituted for the gems we have been touching ever so caressingly.

These minor intuitions often come in clusters, or in a quick succession, but most often without any apparent connection. When we are dreaming awake, or under the influence of music, their number is so great that no calculation can approximate it. We then squander them freely. Yet, we know their value, for, sometimes, they develop into protracted trains of thought, during which we realize that our brain is doing its best work, yet doing it without taxing our coöperation. This is what we want to reproduce after the spell has been interrupted, this is what we call thinking, and the mention of an Art of Thinking means to us chiefly the possibility of recreating at will a similar state of mind. What we call understanding or comprehending is this superior annexation of some intellectual growth. Learning or deducing, as algebra or logic teach us to do, we regard as inferior processes resulting in joyless acquisitions.

4. *Treat intuitions tenderly.* Spiritual books occasionally quote a Latin saying which has terrified more than one soul: *time Jesum transeuntem et non revertentem*: "Dread the passage of Jesus, for He does not return." This amounts to saying: do not let religious intuitions escape you, for they do not come twice.

It is an exaggeration to say that intuitions of any kind never come twice, but they do not come twice with the same appeal. The moment we feel their presence, it is as if we saw the ripple over Bethesda and we ought to know that our chance is near. Silence, both exterior and interior, should prevail; we ought to be attentive but not eager or, above all, curious. The beautiful visitor is like a butterfly, no longer the same when caught. So it must not be caught. If your hand feels for a card and scribbles a few words for fear another thought might displace the first, you will be grateful to yourself, even if you have, many times, to regret the concision forced upon you. But if you are over-wise, and if, in your delight at the visitation, you strive to lose no aspect of it, inserting it forcibly into your intellectual system and greedily noting what it says to you in its rich pregnancy, you will kill it. What is best in Pascal's *Pensées?* Certainly the unfinished parts; the briefer these memos the deeper the vista. La Bruyère would finish his portraits and most of the short essays he has interspersed between them. However, he certainly cared less for those cameos than for the short maxims which he never dared to expand. Writing is one of the methods of relieving the mind, but a desire satisfied is not a desire any more, and it is a pity.

Most French writers cannot put pen to paper without having done what they call—too truly and almost cruelly —thinking *out* their idea. There lies the once living thing, dissected into paragraphs. It cannot be *thought* any more, it can only be written. The vaunted French lucidity is due to that, but what people sometimes call French unpoetical-ness is also due to it. English writers, and even more Russian writers, either feel the presence of their inspiration more deeply, or they are in no such hurry to fix their thoughts, or when they do so their thinking is not over. They do not write because they have thought, they think while writing. Obscurity, congestion, lack of balance are often the consequences. Newman admitted there were passages in his own *Grammar of Assent* which he did not understand. But, what of that, if the writer makes you think, instead of merely teaching you? I believe that French writers are more apt than others to feel the disparity between what they had first conceived and what they actually see between two book covers because of their over-conscious method.

To work on an idea does not mean intellectual concentration of the usual kind. No sweating here will do. A prayerful solitude with a dash of austerity in the daily routine is necessary; then, what Tyndall, describing the production of inventions, called "brooding," and what Newton called "thinking of it all the time." It seems as if the earnest wish to get at the whole thing should be the chief thing, acting, of course, on our subconsciousness. The experience of most artists is that the quality of their production is in keeping with the intensity of their wish. As I said before, Sir Walter Scott reading books with no relevance whatever to his subjects, or Charles Dickens rambling through the deserted streets at night, was trying to retard rather than hasten what we call clear thought, but which ought to be called final thought.

Real work, real brooding consist in peopling the mind with congenial images, sometimes called in by our desire, sometimes conjured up from our memories gone over at random rather than methodically. When the light comes at last, as full as we can expect it ever to be, whatever we do, do not let us map out what we have discovered in the shape of a synopsis. Numbering and brackets are too unlike thought ever to revive its first appearance.

5. *Cultivate evocative moods.* There is in us a stratum more sensitive than the rest, which we know and where we can go at will. A behaviorist would say that the inevitability of the response from that stratum in our consciousness proves that it is biological, but all I want to say

is that we know from experience that the response is sure. If we live a great deal with ourselves we increase our personality, and if we revive certain facts or periods, or phases of feeling in our lives, we heighten our receptivity.

Our life with its peaks—which we know—of sentiment, effort, nobility, or increased intelligence, is a veritable mine of evocative moods. A few minutes' leisure is enough to re-place ourselves in such moods, and no sooner are we conscious of them than the phosphorescence of intuitive-ness begins. Poets know it well. Their own experience, some-times woefully restricted in appearance, is the constant sup-port of their inspiration. They, as well as artists, are re-markably like children, and have never broken the thread binding the various periods of their lives together, as men living in the world, and for the world, will do. Their childhood especially, with its wealth and depth of impres-sions, is frequently present to them. Nothing is more evoca-tive than the memory of early years. What narrative of a childhood, from *David Copperfield* to *Du Côté de chez Swann,* does not delight us, even when the novelist or memorialist has not the power of a Dickens or a Proust? The reason is that all the impressions recorded are fresh, and connect at once with the freshest ones we possess. Life, in time, wrenches us from those memories to mind what we call our fights, which are, in most cases, anything but noble, but even very young people realize their value to themselves. I used to know a schoolboy who, before tackling an essay, would go back to his childish emo-tions or griefs, and imagined he found himself at once in the productive part of his soul.

Some faraway states of consciousness, difficult to define at the time, because they were so rich, and never quite exhausted in spite of frequent drawing upon them, still preserve their haunting quality and evocative power. I shall never quite account for the fact that long before visiting

Spain I felt something Spanish in the atmosphere of the Good Friday of a year when I was nine or ten. The same *éclat,* the same impassioned violence. Later on, an afternoon of All Souls' Day filled me with the same wondering excitement which, even now, I can renew at a few minutes' notice. It was a brilliant November afternoon, apparently ill-suited to the melancholy of the day; the heavens were high and deep. An east wind was blowing its mad exhilaration through the park avenues, themselves all sunny and lyrical. From one kingly aspen thousands of golden leaves seemed to leap into the blue, little souls released, at last, and plunging into infinity. The château had not been deserted for Paris, yet, but its inmates were not abroad, and I was the only living person looking at the gorgeous sight. I felt as if I possessed it all with all its magic, as if the mystery of Autumn's beauty were solved at last; yet, I should have been unable to analyze the scene and its effect upon me.

Who cannot remember such moments, and who, remembering them, does not realize that he is where his soul is the most active, although it does nothing to break its passivity? Such experiences, renewed when we wish, do more than years of conscious effort or laborious study to teach us what thought is and where it is.

Chapter Fifteen

LITERARY PRODUCTION POSSIBLE TO ALL

"Literary production possible to all . . . You want us to be writers like yourself, don't you?—Or, do you feel that writing is the only way to reach perfection in thinking?"

"Far be it from me to wish for such a thing! If I could reduce printed matter to one-thousandth of what it is, I should do it in a second. And if there is a melancholy object it is the man or woman trying to write, as others try to sing, or paint, or act, or do anything, without talent."

"Well then, what is that marvellous literary production which, being possible to all, is therefore possible to me? How can I wriggle myself into the history of literature without adding to that mountain of printed matter which you say you dislike?"

"Do you regard all that is in print as literature?"

"What a question! Ask me another."

"Then do you think that all that has a right to be called literature is in print?"

"No, O Socrates, I do not. Every day we hear of famous writers' unpublished manuscripts being discovered. They were literature from the moment they were written, I should think. Year after year we hear that somebody's correspondence or somebody's memoirs have just been discovered and are going to be printed. I suppose those memoirs and letters are literature, and were so even in manuscript."

"Yes, Madame de Sévigné's or Chesterfield's letters are in every textbook, and so are Saint-Simon's memoirs, and so is Pepys' diary, and so are hundreds and hundreds of collections of letters or memoirs by less known authors who, however, cannot be left out of what we call literature. Why?"

"Well written, I suppose."

"But what is good writing?"

"Why, distinguished language, or witty language, or noble, or touching, or in any way fascinating language. Whatever is high above the common run of what we all write is well written, I should think."

"Excellent! You realize there is a distinction to be made between mere words and the sentiments they express. If Jeanne d'Arc, who certainly was no scholar, had left a correspondence, it would be literature, no doubt."

"Why! If Tommy Jones' love-letters to Miss Brown were revealed they would be literature. He once showed one to me and I turned green with envy. Yet, Jones is no writer, bless him."

"You mean that every deep or strong sentiment, faithfully expressed, is literature. And so it is. That is why we all love letters so, and read them as greedily fifty years after they were written as the maid of fifty years ago did when she found them on madame's desk. We hate egotism, but somehow we love to hear people talk about themselves."

"Do you . . . do you think my letters are literature?"

"Some of your letters must have been. But those which you write to me nowadays are certainly not. You never say a word about what you think or feel, you tell me what you do or what other people do, but you never analyze either your own, or their motives as you would, as in fact you constantly do, while discussing people in the smoking-room. Your letters are full of trivialities and full of clichés. Surely Jones' letter to Miss Brown did not look like that."

"I am afraid you are right, even if you are discouraging. But shall I tell you why I write that kind of letter, why we all write the same letter, all the time? Well, business does that. You get used to dictating twenty times over the same letter to different people, and in time your mind cannot get away from the business rhythm. I write to my wife as I do to you, and she used to complain about it. Now she does not. She is used to it, I suppose."

"You've hit the nail on the head this time. When I say that we all can produce literature in our letters I mean that a letter gives us a unique chance of expressing our self. Nobody is reading it over our shoulder, nobody is expected to criticize it after it is written. In the terms used in this book, no phantasm is to be feared, no inferiority complex is likely to weaken us. We are at our best to express what we know best, namely the feelings immediately perceptible to our consciousness. This ought to result in absolute naturalness, which is literature. I know a novelist, a woman, whose books are painful reading. The poor dear is never herself. She is Sinclair Lewis one year, Willa Cather the next, that is to say she tries to be, but only produces cheap imitations like an Oklahoma seamstress trying to copy Paris styles. But the same woman writes letters in which you see her life and her soul in a transparent light, every word acting like a bright little bulb instead of a dull little patch."

"Oh, I know what you mean, of course, but why should I write literature?"

"Nobody wants you to write literature. What I object to is waste. Every day you waste a chance, many chances in fact, of getting at your innermost consciousness by expressing yourself as you see yourself, and I say it is a pity because it makes you, year after year and day after day, more like anybody else and more anonymous. Mind you, you may have more strength, or what you call strength, today than when you left college, but you had more individuality at twenty-one than now. You were nearer to yourself and nearer to good books, that is to say, to a standard of satisfactory expression. Indeed, like most people, you wrote a much better letter in those days. You have hardened and ossified from mere laziness resulting in rather shameful imitation. You have to bear your share of the blame for hearing the same conversation ten times over if you go to ten different places. Literature is self-expression, I tell you, and self-expression is individuality, and our individuality is our self, which ought to be our chief concern. But we enrich that poor self of ours all our lives with money, and all our lives we impoverish it by stealing from it what makes it our self till there is nothing left. The language is only too accurate when it speaks of nobodies or ciphers. The world is a huge number consisting of a few figures and of an astronomical row of noughts. Therefore, stiffen, resist, say no, for heaven's sake, and if you do, you will be a real man and your letters will be real letters which might be printed as so many have been."

"I will make a note of all this. It is worth it, and I dare say it is what you call literature."

"Let literature alone, but by all means make notes. If you would note all that you hear or think that you feel is worth remembering, the collection would be a valuable diary. Read Amiel's Diary, it will not bore you, and you will see what can happen in a life spent in a little Swiss town in which apparently nothing ever happened. Packed full with the only things that count: thoughts and sentiments."

"Well, I am willing to produce literature of the kind you describe, but how I should hate to appear in print!"

"I know. You only print the balance-sheet of your bank. That is enough, and lots of people think it capital reading.

But let me assure you that innumerable writers whose books you hear mentioned possessed less capacity for reading their own consciousness or expressing it than many men of whom destiny made bankers."

To sum up, everyone of us can be personal, that is to say, creative, if he is not in danger of losing his personality in self-consciousness, or through the phantasms besetting whoever tries to express himself. This means that he, at once, becomes interesting to his fellow-beings and indifferent only to an individual who will drown himself in the multitude. This interest is the basis of literature, and so, it is obvious that we all can produce what has a right to be called literature, but we must not be thinking of literature while doing so. The doctrine underlying this volume is that thought alone counts, and thought cannot coexist with anything that is not our self in its highest and noblest possibility.

CONCLUSION

THIS BOOK has not been written for literary people although it had to be based on a writer's experience. Nothing could be farther removed from its purpose than a tendency to regard the thinker as a specialist instead of as merely a man worthy of the name. The author feels deep respect for any man in possession of high principles which speak through his conduct as well as through his words. Whatever may be his deficiencies this man is a thought incarnate.

Give such a person the means of strengthening his thinking capacity by broadening the field and raising the level of his thought, and you will make him and his influence proportionately greater. Show him the possibility of attaining to Vision or Creativeness, and you lift him up to the supreme height.

This is what this book is trying to do. It cannot produce the wish to think where it does not exist, but, given this indispensable germ, it ought to provide the necessary conditions to bring it to maturity. Ask men who have developed what started them on their progress. You will often be surprised by the simplicity as well as by the variety of their answers. A few words in a book, the catalog of a school, the mere outline of a method, the impression left by an exceptional man, his reaction to intelligence or to fatuity, the expression of his face, his very silences, may have been enough.

A similar effect can be produced or, at all events, prepared, by some random sentence in pages full as these are of a desire to help thought. To some people the advice: "Read the newspaper as a page of history," will sound like an epigram. But to others it may be the starting point of a new mental life. Others again may be helped by the mere rhythm of this work, by its Contents, or by its title alone.

Here, as in other things, what is wanted is a beginning and a method. The beginning belongs to God, but the method belongs to us, and it can be learned, in a few hours, even from such a book as this. The writer has had no other ambition and he cherishes no greater hope than that of being useful.

INDEX

INDEX

INDEX

INDEX

OUTSTANDING PAPERBACKS FROM FAWCETT PREMIER

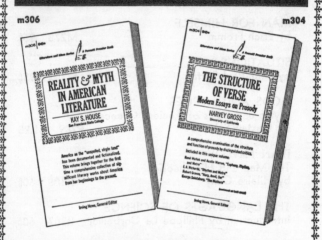